ANGLING FOR A LIFE

Angling for a Life

Tony Curnow

The Pentland Press Limited
Edinburgh · Cambridge · Durham · USA

First published in 2000 by
The Pentland Press Ltd.
1 Hutton Close
South Church
Bishop Auckland
Durham

British Library Cataloguing in Publication Data.
A catalogue record for this book is available
from the British Library.

ISBN 1 85821 829 2

Typeset by George Wishart & Associates, Whitley Bay.
Printed and bound by Antony Rowe Ltd., Chippenham

To my sister Christine, for her strength and encouragement, and to Sophie and Kathryn.

CHAPTER 1

January 31st 1949. What a great day that was for an unsuspecting world. At approximately 3.05 a.m. a tiny wrinkled red head popped out from its mother's womb and proceeded to shock nursing staff and mother with its screams of derision and helplessness. So helpless did that baby feel on that day that it tried in vain to stay where it was, until a pair of stainless steel forceps managed eventually to prise it from the comfort and warmth of its donor.

'By Christ!' said the midwife, 'He's an ugly little bastard isn't he! And what a frigging racket he's making.'

Ugly I may have been but the aforementioned racket emitting from my lungs that cold horrible morning had nothing to do with the fact that I had just been plucked from the security of the womb. The truth was I had just taken in my first view of Port Clarence and for the next seventeen years this was to be my home.

Port Clarence 1949

'When Irish eyes are smiling, sure they're all as pissed as farts.'

The lullabies that my Irish grandma used to sing to me still haunt me to this day. My grandad had elephant feet, round ones with funny little toes and as I remember he never used to sing lullabies to me. I never got on with my grandad, he took an instant dislike to me and used to use me for football practice just in case he got a call up from the Boro.

Port Clarence is situated to the north of Middlesbrough and at that time I suppose it must have been eighty per cent Irish Roman Catholic, hence the lullabies from grandma. The school was Roman Catholic, the Church was Roman Catholic and do you know, people say remember the good old days. They certainly were days gone by but as for being good, what a load of shite!

Separating Port Clarence from Middlesbrough is the Transporter Bridge which still stands to this day as an epitaph to the steelworkers and construction workers of Irish descent who erected it. In my late adolescence, which my daughter Kathryn still thinks I am going through, we, as a gang used to scramble over this monolith late at night to procure young pigeons straight from the nest to build up our lofts on the local allotments. Oblivious to the dangers that this represented at the time, as you do, when you're young, we built up a considerable number of these birds and at a later date we would use their feathers as lures whilst fishing for mackerel from the Heugh Breakwater at Hartlepool. Our family grew and grew and you could tell that my Dad was never on night shift. The production line eventually stopped at eight and my siblings consisted of two sisters and five brothers none of whom I expect made as much noise as I when first setting eyes upon the dismal poverty that was Port Clarence.

The local school, Roman Catholic of course, sported five classrooms, each with about forty pupils and each with an ogre for a teacher except as I remember the infants class. I can't remember the teacher's name but what I can remember as a seven year old is that I didn't want to leave the security of her beauty and calmness. There was many a time whilst pretending to be ill, that I would sit on her lap and snuggle up to her, breathing in her perfume with my head between her ample tits, the old one eyed trouser snake doing curious things even at that tender age.

The school also sported a woodwork room overseen by that old master Willy Trodden who had a passion, a deep passion, for twatting you over the head with your poor exhibition of carpentering skills. It was in this classroom that I tried to assemble my first fishing rod with absolutely diabolical results. With old pot bellied stoves that were fed on coke the classrooms gave off an awful aroma during the winter months fuelled on fumes from the coke, Vick, that had been rubbed on many a pupil's chest the night before and wellington boots. Do you know, we wore wellington boots all the time when I look back. You used to get tide marks around your calves where the wellies slapped against them even during the summer months. Being a coke monitor, a milk monitor and an ink monitor I had managed to acquire a few cushy numbers here, as jack the lad you had to take full advantage. If I could count the number of bras that I have had my dirty little hand into when I was supposed to be filling up stoves or inkwells or dishing out bottles of creamy milk, Berlei would take me on now as an experienced consultant. The only good thing that came from my school days I have to admit, is that it led me into fishing, a sport that even now I still get a tingle about, especially when I think about my head between those big tits.

With four in a bed, two at the top and two at the bottom, the last thing that we wanted in our bed was another body but unfortunately when my youngest brother Paul was born that is exactly what we got. So, we had five in the bed and the big one said, 'scratch me back'. Oh it was bliss. I used to pick on one of them and threaten them with a good hiding. 'Scratch me back,' I used to say, 'or I'll thump ya!!!' Do you know I had my first sexual experience in life in that bed, our Stewart pissed up me back!!!

I will never forget the time that my Mam and Dad invited a couple back to our house after they had spent the night together in the old Royal public house. We heard them come in and as you do I shouted, 'Mam, can I come down.'

'Go to sleep!' was the stern reply.

'Mam, our Tony's pulling the greatcoat over him and we can't get warm.'

'It's not a greatcoat,' came the embarrassed answer, 'it's an eiderdown.'

Several minutes later came the reply, 'Mam, the arm's just fell off the eiderdown.'

It was about this time of life when those dark hairs start to sprout from your nether regions and you start to get those twitchings down below and you don't exactly know what your old tallywhacker is doing.

'Ragworm is the best bait you can get,' said someone on a rather auspicious occasion when we, as a gang were verbally experimenting the ins and outs of female anatomy. 'Naw, it's a fact,' he said 'Ragworm is better than lug.'

Now as a lover of the promotion of the one eyed knicker viper up any unsuspecting stocking clad leg, a little bit of mystery had occurred here and I was in some doubt as to exactly what the fuck a lugworm was. Was it something that kept the knickers up or something that crawled out of their arses once a month? As it turned out the lugworm as a bait was one of my greatest baits for one of my greatest captures. But enough about that for now. Something had got me hooked into fishing. Something had pulled me, so to speak from bashing the bishop into bashing the fish. A subtle difference but in many ways the smell was the same. It was like something had gripped me, not by the bollocks exactly but something very akin to it. What the fuck was a lugworm, what the fuck was a ragworm?

Sea fishing 1959

During the war years, the army used to use part of the north east coast for its billets for the poor embittered army, training for the great struggle across the sea and of course as any great army does it left behind its mementoes: torpedoes, hand grenades, clips of .303 ammunition. Oh aye lad we found them all whilst digging for lugworm and ragworm. We used to collect it by the bucketful, ten lugworm, one clip of bullets, ten ragworm, one torpedo. Where now stands the massive expanse of the Seal Sands oil and chemical industry, used to stand the best sea bait area in the North East of England. There used to be a host of house boats along the creek that fed into the North Sea there. The people that inhabited them in the summer months are I suppose gone now and it is still very, very nostalgic today when I drive over that bridge and see the decaying stumps of what once used to be a very happy place. But anyway, we used to dig for bait there and along the creek and into the bay that now hosts the nuclear power station.

Oh how times have changed. We used to pile onto the Hartlepool bus with our dads' wellies on with the Wimpey logos on the side. We used to pick fag ends up and smoke them into oblivion and threaten anyone that came near us with our garden forks and spades. We would gather a bucketful of shiny red and black ragworm and deep black lugworm and then we would go home and prepare for the night's fishing. We would board the last bus which was inevitably full of drunks who smoked a lot and left big tab ends on the floor for us youngsters to grab and to share later on as we rerolled them into Rizla papers. Sometimes we would get a flash of stockinged leg as an amorous hand led its merry way up a drunken thigh and if we were really really lucky sometimes an enormous white breast would appear during a rendition of Danny Boy.

'Where are we going tonight then?' someone would ask as we piled off the bus laden with a huge assortment of vintage and decrepit fishing tackle.

'We'll start at the red light and then when the tide comes in a bit we'll go around to the Heugh, eh,' said someone else. What a rather splendid idea that seemed but to be truthful it didn't matter where we went, we were fishing. The red light in fact, is situated just north of Old Hartlepool docks and the life boat as I recall used to sit proudly on the jetty there. As the clock at St Hilda's church struck midnight, we would be about ready and by this time most of our strawberry jam sandwiches would have been consumed. We had to secure a spot along the jetty and having obtained our place it was a matter then of setting up our tackle.

Now as fishing tackle goes this highly original collection of piscatorial weaponry left a lot to be desired. Fashioned from anything that even resembled a fishing rod it was as dangerous as it was cumbersome but as a young lad it was your pride and joy. My rod had been made from a six-foot length of bamboo cane into which I had whipped some line guides and an old rusting Penn reel. I used to employ a rather soft cast that would send out my terminal tackle into the dark inky waters and as a casting weight I would use a few old nuts. We would catch whiting and billet, dabs and flounders and by morning would have a carrier bag full of fish to take home. The journey home would be a very tired, subdued affair and we used to share the early bus with the workmen who hawked and brought up phlegm from their chests. We would swap a couple of whiting for a woodbine and eventually arrive home completely and utterly knackered.

Most of our misspent youth centred around fishing and in a way our parents would be glad to see the carrier bag full of fish. It sometimes decided whether or not the family ate that day. We constantly updated our equipment and eventually we would be making our own lead weights from molten lead acquired by any means. There weren't many lead overflow pipes left around Port Clarence. We would melt the lead in an old baked bean can over the gas stove and then pour it steadily into a large dessert spoon. The gas was metered in those days and to obtain any supply you had to put a shilling into the meter. Now being as poor as poor could be a shilling was a lot of money so we used to file down an old halfpenny until it fitted perfectly into the slot.

'Shunting poles,' said someone one day. 'Shunting poles from off the railway will make great fishing rods.'

As we sat there smoking a Woodbine or two our minds drifted away from the naked ladies pictured in the book that we had found and our thoughts started to compile various ways of how to convert shunting poles into fishing rods. The stiffness inside our underpants disappeared as swiftly as the discarded book as we swapped ideas on how to tackle this new project.

'Let's ask Willie Trodden if we can make them in the woodwork class,' said someone, and so for the next few months our carpentry and joinery skills would be put to the test. When the school was eventually knocked down I suppose that my rod was still there stood beside the gluepot. My parents could ill afford to buy me the necessary brass ferrules or the line guides and a young lad's dream was shattered.

Ringworm and nits were an occupational hazard in Port Clarence as were hunger and desperation. Even today if you travel the road that leaves Port Clarence towards Hartlepool you won't see many fencing posts along the road side. They were all burnt on domestic fires to keep the houses warm. Any potato crop that appeared in the fields around Port Clarence was swiftly demolished and we would feast for months on chips and whiting, chips and billet and chips and dab.

We had a huge gang the most famous of whom I suppose was Joe Tasker. To those of you who have ever read any of Chris Bonnington's books on his conquest of Everest, you may have read about Joe. He left our school at about 14 years of age as I recall, to go to train to be a priest. Years later whilst reading the

8

book, Joe's name was mentioned and to be honest I did think that it was a coincidence until I saw the photograph of Joe. Joe's body is still up there to this day. After an attempt on the summit of Everest, Joe and his companion were never seen alive again but I do believe that his companion's body was found some years ago.

Our parents tried desperately to bring us all up in a dignified way which in some ways was nigh on impossible. Saturday night was always bath night in our house and after I had returned from bait digging, that scrubbing brush which my Mam wielded was an instrument of eternal torture. The old tin bath would be dragged out and pans and kettles of boiling water would be constantly on the go refilling it. The nit comb would come out and as she dragged it through your hair you would scream with agony. After being deloused and rubbed dry with a coarse towel it would be time to reapply the purple ointment onto the ringworm. It stained the affected area horribly, everyone knew that you had ringworm.

Every Sunday morning saw us kids all holding hands as we set off for the 10.30 mass at St Thomas's church. We would have patches on our clothing and cardboard box insoles in our shoes in an attempt to stop the damp seeping through the holes in them. With purple patches on our legs and a Woodbine nicked from my Dad's packet in my pocket, we would enter through those holy doors. That is all but I. With a quick about turn I was back out of those doors and a quick turn to the left brought me around to the back of the church where I would sit with my fag constantly lighting it and then nipping it out. Inside, the mainly female choir would be thundering out those hymns that I still remember today. The church would be packed with every pew full, males on the right, headscarved females on the left.

I hated school and hated having to go to church. I would much rather have been fishing or bait collecting. My Mam had to get used to my constant pleading for any spare cash but the reality was there just wasn't any. I remember once when my Dad, having been out of work for a while, set off one Sunday night to walk to Newcastle to start a new job the following morning. For two weeks he slept rough and eventually walked all the way back with two weeks wages in his pocket. If it wasn't for the carrier bag full of fish and hand outs from caring neighbours I don't know how we would have survived.

He is a proud man my dad, ex Chief Petty Officer in the Royal Navy, ex Police Constable and former General Foreman on the construction sites. He is at 76 years of age, still working full time in an old people's home, many of whom are younger than him. Throughout those long summer holidays however when the sun seemed constantly to shine we would escape the slum conditions and descend upon Seaton Carew or Seaton Snooks. We would fish and collect bait. We would walk throughout the night between the Heugh and the red light and on one particular occasion, having just set off between locations and in between a lull in the conversation we heard a sort of shuffling, groaning sound.

'What the fuck's that?' someone said.

'It might be a fucking ghost,' whispered someone else . . .

'Cmon it's coming from over there,' someone else whispered. As we approached the beach the hairs on the back of my neck stood on end. As we peered through the gloom we could see something moving, furiously going up and down. At that moment the bank of cloud that had been obscuring the moon drifted away and what we saw was a little white arse going up and down and two people obviously in the deep throes of passion.

'Cmon,' someone whispered and as we crept forward the little white arse moved faster and faster.

'OOOOH!' cried the lady. 'AAAAGH!' cried the gent and that was when I smacked his arse.

'You little bastards!' He screamed as he tried to run after us with his trousers around his ankles. His tallywhacker was swinging between his legs and it was obvious that his night of passion was over. We last saw him trying to chase after her shouting, 'Come back, they've fucked off now,' and then as she disappeared into the night clutching her knickers, 'You little bastaaaaards!'

The fishing continued amidst the zits and spots of adolescence and then came that fateful horrible day when at fifteen years of age we were kicked out of school and told to make our own way in life from then on. It is a sign of changing years and attitudes but on leaving school every one of us secured an apprenticeship of some sort. The Haverton Hill shipyard was in its prime in those days and most of my fellow class mates secured jobs as welders or burners. As my dad was a foreman on the building sites he managed to get me a job as an apprentice joiner and what fucking fun I had with that job for the next two and a half years.

To start work on the sites you obviously had to have hard boots and so on the Saturday prior to me starting with CM Yuills my dad went to sort the job out. He must have been pissed because he came home with a pair of boots one of which had eight lace holes in and the other six lace holes. Greenwoods pawnbrokers in Middlesbrough was the shop where he had purchased the boots and as it was now 5.30 the shop would be shut and there was no possible way to exchange them. My dad had also purchased for me a large blue duffle coat with a hood attached to it and as I had no haversack I used to carry my sandwiches in the hood. The lads on the site christened me the Lunchbox of Amsterdam.

I wouldn't say that the lads were rough but one day in deepest darkest January, when the snow lay two feet thick on the ground, two joiners picked me up and upended me before smashing the ice with my head and finally dropping me head first into one of the brickies 45 gallon oil drums that contained the water for the cement mixer. The bastards used to nail me to the inside of cupboard doors and if I had been really mean they would coat me in emulsion paint from head to toe and kick me out of the bait room with no clothes on. Which isn't the right thing to do to a Port lad. Oh no, payback time was always relished and when it happened I gloated boyishly. I used to nail their haversacks to roofing joists and slip sugar into their petrol tanks. I would let all the tyres down on the works bus or on their private cars.

11

'What have you got in your sandwiches?' the scots JCB driver said to me one day.

'Jam,' I answered.

'Would ye like to swap one?' he said.

'What have you got then?' I asked.

'Porridge,' he said. Now I ask you, I though jam butties were a bit, well poorish, but *porridge* sandwiches!

One good plus point about working on the sites was the amount of spare lead that lay about. Now having purchased a sinker mould that could produce lead weights up to 6oz this was the biz. The hood on the duffelcoat used to be full every night, the only trouble was I usually ended up staring at the stars as the weight of the lead dragged my head back. The amount of dog shit that I stood in whilst going through this phase was nobody's business. But the good thing about working for a living is that you get paid and when you get paid you could buy Woodbines, although No 6 with the filter tips were just coming on the scene. You could also buy fishing gear and old Greenwoods pawnbrokers got some stick from me. Scarborough reels and great big fuck off beachcasters. Proper silver hooks without a trace of rust and all the other paraphernalia associated with fishing. I even had a proper box to keep it all in and the fishing certainly improved. We would still dig for bait on a Saturday at the mudflats under the Seal Sands complex and little did I know then that these same mudflats would nearly claim my life years later. We would have casting competitions and as the terminal tackle sped out seaward a voice shouted, 'Look out Hitler, that bastard's going to land in Germany.'

One dark Saturday evening as the drizzle came down and we huddled together puffing on No 6, the bell that was attached to my rod end tinkled. 'Fucking crabs!' I said as I gave the rod a mighty whoop. 'Fuck me, it isn't a crab this,' I shouted and to my amazement I hauled up an enormous flatty.

'What the fuck's that,' said someone. It turned out to be a Dover sole of huge proportions that had fancied a lugworm for its supper that night. I often wondered how a Dover sole had managed to get lost from the Kent coastline and end up in Hartlepool of all places. I mean, this is the place where they hang monkeys you know . . .

Suddenly a great change came over our lives as the hormones swept through us. We finally found to our enjoyment just exactly what the meat and two veg were for – and we discovered booze. Money that should have been used wisely for fishing ended behind the bar of the Billingham Arms. We used to drink black velvets or cider. In fact we would drink anything. We wore suits now, you know the ones with no collars just like the Beatles did. We wore winklepickers and chisel toes shoes and grew our hair long. Then a new phase swept the gang, motor bikes: there were BSA Bantams and Triumph Tiger Cubs, AJS and Vellocette. There were Bonervilles and Nortons and the deaths that go with them. Some of the lads that I had grown up with never made it past seventeen, smashed to bits on some lonely road late at night. I thank the Lord that I wasn't one of them. Money was still tight however, we never seemed to have enough of it and so one day I asked my dad if he could wangle a pay rise for me but obviously he couldn't. Now as an apprentice you had to work with tradesmen and in most cases these men would have a target to work to and if they exceeded the target they qualified for some bonus. The two joiners that I worked with exceeded their targets every week but would they give me a backhander – no they certainly wouldn't – but it was unofficial site policy that the apprentices received some sort of financial inducement. The case dragged on for weeks but they just didn't want to part with any loot at all. The site that we worked on at the time was the massive Mowden Park residential estate in Darlington and seeing as my dad was one of the foremen I thought that maybe, just maybe, something would happen. It did, but not in the way that I had planned. My dad had said to me one Thursday evening as he lay on his sick bed, 'Look son, I can't do anything about it, you will have to see Mr Brown.'

Now Mr Brown was the site agent and like a demigod to us

mere lads so I thought that I had better have a drop of Dutch courage before I spoke with him. Courage beer it was, funnily enough, and after four pints I went back to see him. He was talking to two potential buyers at the time and I asked quietly, 'Excuse me, Mr Brown, could I have a word please.'

'GET OUT OF MY OFFICE, BOY!' he hurled back and like a sheep I trudged wearily through the door. Having reached the fresh air, I thought, now hang on a minute, who's he talking to.

'Can I have a word, Mr Brown.'

'I'VE TOLD YOU ONCE,' he said prodding my chest with a nicotine stained finger. 'GET OUT OF MY OFFICE.'

The punch that I threw took him straight off his feet and as he stood up with blood trickling from his mouth, ran to the back of his desk for protection and screamed, 'GET OUT, GET OUT, YOU'RE SACKED.'

Six weeks later the powers that be called me into head office and explained the errors of my ways and said that as an indentured apprentice what a fool I had been. If I apologised here and now, I could have my job back . . .

'FAAARCK OFF,' I replied and two minutes later I was outside of the building clutching six weeks back pay and my cards. As I walked along York Road in Hartlepool I came across the Naval recruitment office and I thought, right, this is the place for me. I walked through the door and spotted this guy in what I thought was an Army uniform. 'Have I got the wrong place?' I asked.

'Who are you looking for, son?' he said.

'The Royal fucking Navy,' I answered as hard as I could.

'Well you've come to the right place,' he said smiling.

'Well who the fuck are you then?' I asked.

'Have you ever heard of the Royal Marines son,' he asked, still smiling.

'What the fuck's one of them?' I asked.

'Well come over here,' he said, 'and take a chair and I'll tell you all about it.'

The destruction of HMS Repulse

The battle ship HMS *Prince of Wales* accompanied by the battle cruiser HMS *Repulse* steamed north off the north east coast of Malaya on December 8th 1941. The previous day the American Pacific fleet had been severely damaged by over 300 Japanese planes at the Hawaii base of Pearl Harbour. The flanking destroyers of these two capital ships, bristling with AA guns darted and dashed in their never ending display of power and speed as their respective young Captains tried to outdo each other. With no air cover, as had been expected, this force was at best pregnable and the sad events that occurred later that day proved that in modern warfare the use of covering air support is essential. Having found no Japanese landings, as had been reported, the flotilla returned south to engage another reported Japanese landing force at Kota Baru. At around midnight a torpedo bomber group of the Imperial Japanese Air Force located the ships and proceeded immediately to attack. HMS *Repulse* was hit by five torpedoes and at 12.33 a.m. she was sunk. About forty five minutes later HMS *Prince of Wales* was also sunk. 503 men from HMS *Repulse* were lost in this action and over 300 men from the *Prince of Wales*. My father was one of the survivors.

CHAPTER 2

Royal Marines 1966 to 1976

I stepped from the train at Deal in Kent a very lonely and frightened boy. Throughout the journey from Middlesbrough Railway Station, I had had plenty of time to reflect on my life so far and my opinion was that I hadn't really had a life. But as I stood there, a forlorn little seventeen year old boy, I would have given anything to be back home. I spotted the Lance Corporal so smart in his Lovat uniform with the green beret perched cockily on his head. I drew myself up to my full height of five feet fuck all and spread my leather clad shoulders as wide as I could. He seemed to be scrutinising me as he stood there and I don't for one minute expect that he was impressed with what he saw: a long haired spotty faced youth clad in ice blue skin tight jeans who stood there atop a pair of 2 inch high winklepicker boots. The studs on the back of the leather jacket said 'Death to the Mods' and supporting the skin tight ice blue jeans was a heavy leather belt also covered in metal studs. The carrier bag that held my personal possessions smelt vaguely of fish but the Lance Corporal didn't seem to notice as he said 'NAME?'

'Curnow'...

His eyebrows twitched slightly.

'CURNOW WHAT' he shouted.

Aye up, I thought, am I supposed to call this twat something.

'Curnow, your worship' I answered.

The eyebrows twitched again.

'WHEN YOU ADDRESS A NON COMMISSIONED OFFICER IN THE ROYAL MARINES, YOU WILL ADDRESS HIM BY HIS RANK!' he shouted.

'All right,' I said, 'Keep your fucking hair on,' and then I noticed that he didn't have any. I arrived at the barracks in Deal in the rear of a land rover together with another guy who had arrived on the same train as I. The Lance Comical led us into an office and introduced us to a huge bear of a man who had a similar hair cut.

'Curnow and Coles, Sarn't Major,' said the Lance Comical.

'Hello lads,' said this grizzled old bear, 'Would you like a cup of tea, go and make us all a nice cuppa will you Corp,' he said, and as the Lance Comical walked away I raised my index finger proudly behind his back.

The rest of the evening was taken up by trying to make a bed properly after an introduction from our 'Squad Instructor', another Lance Comical but this time he had two golden stripes on his arm, whatever that meant. Other guys drifted in from every part of the country imaginable and by about nine thirty two more Lance Comicals appeared and explained what tomorrow held for us. 'You will have to get up I'm afraid at six o'clock, and then you will have to make your own beds and sweep the room out. The cleaners are on strike you see, but anyway, we'll come to collect you at 7.30 and we'll all go to breakfast, OK lads . . . see you in the morning.'

'Fuck me, this is a bit of all right,' I thought but as soon as I lay my head down some daft twat started to blow a bugle. Everyone started to get up so I followed suit and dragged my way to the shower block. Having made our beds and swept up as instructed the two Lance Comicals came back and the bigger one said, 'Fall in outside lads.' What the fuck did he mean, but like the rest I followed the two NCOs out of the door. They tried to assemble into some sort of formation, very quietly mind you and soon we were marching to breakfast. We halted outside and they led us into the dining hall.

What awaited us was something that I have never experienced in my life before, 500 skinheads with their knives and forks at the ready started to drum as loudly as they could on to the table tops. The noise was deafening and I could just

17

make out the Corporal's words when he said 'Welcome to the Royal Marines.'

After breakfast they led us into a large lecture room and told us that an Officer was coming to see us and that we all had to sign some papers. The Officer duly arrived and he explained the joining procedure. 'Does anyone want to go home before you sign?' he said. Two lads got up and walked out and then the Officer said 'OK, if you will all sign your papers and pass them to the front.' Having completed the necessary tasks the Officer seemed to be counting the papers and checking them over. 'They are all yours, Sergeant,' he said quietly.

So engrossed had we been with the paperwork that we hadn't noticed a group of camouflaged suits sneak in behind us. 'STAND UP, GET OUTSIDE AND FALL IN IN THREE RANKS, MOVE MOVE MOVE' . . .

Training at the Depot

For me my angling career had come to an abrupt halt and for the following months fishing was the last thing on my mind.

They marched us into the barbers. 'SIX AT A TIME, MOVE, MOVE, MOVE!'

They stood there, six demon barbers with their electric shears buzzing.

'What were you before you joined up?' asked the barber of the lad who was in front of me.

'A shepherd,' he answered.

When I sat in the seat he said, 'What were you, one of his fucking sheep?'

We ran and ran. We saluted and polished and for months on end we didn't quite know really where we were. They cajoled us, bollocked us and turned us from being daft civvies into something resembling a soldier. During those months of eternal hardship and whilst running around the camp I had noticed another guy who was vaguely familiar and although his hair was as short as mine you could tell that it was blond. Barry Clapp, the man who was christened the world's ugliest angler by Mac Campbell many years later and the man who I shared many, many experiences with, some too tragic even to recall now.

They taught us how to wash clothes and how to stitch and darn. They showed us how to iron clothes and shine boots so that you could see your face in them. They drilled us on the parade ground and taught us how to throw hand grenades and they fed us three times a day with real food . . .

Then came that great day when the instructors thought that we were competent enough to hold a rifle.

'THAT'S THE END WHERE THE BULLETS COME OUT OF,

19

CURNOW, AND THAT'S THE END THAT YOU STICKS INTO YOUR SHOULDER,' said the Corporal as he turned my rifle around.

'Fuck me,' I thought. 'This is better than my old .177 Diana back home.' We were instructed in the use of the 7.62mm SLR and practised and practised with it.

'FORGET YOUR COCKS NOW,' shouted the instructors. 'FROM NOW ON YOUR RIFLE IS YOUR BEST MATE.'

To this day I have never pulled my best mate through with a piece of four by two and I have never, ever tweaked his fore sight with a matchstick.

Shore Leave

Being part of the Royal Navy a lot of the internal language of this great service is similar and so when you go out of the camp on an evening, it's called shore leave, even though you're not afloat. So anyway, there we were preparing to go ashore into Deal for our first spot of leave. We had shaved the bum fluff from our chins and splattered liberal helpings of Old Spice everywhere.

'The first thing I'm going to do,' said someone, 'is have a fucking good shag and then ten pints of beer followed by a curry.'

The reality of it was that we had about as much chance of getting ashore as a rat did running through the streets of Port Clarence. We first of all had to get past the Guardroom ... There is something that happens to certain individuals when a stripe is put on their arms that turns them into right twats and in that Guardroom is where they all lived. I stood there in front of this pillock who walked around and around me for about five minutes.

'I can smell perfume,' he whispered into my ear. 'Are you wearing perfume lad?'

'No corporal,' I answered.

'YOU ARE WEARING PERFUME,' he spluttered and little bits of spittle splattered my face. 'Are you a brown hatter?' he said quietly.

'What's a brown hatter, Corporal?' I said.

His face lit up. 'YOU DON'T KNOW WHAT A BROWN HATTER IS LAD.'

'No Corporal' ...

'WELL REPORT TO MY BEDSPACE AT TEN O'CLOCK IN SHIRT TAIL ORDER AND I'LL SHOW YOU!' he screamed. With the peak of his hat touching his nose he stared at me and I stared back. I was just about to nut him when the telephone rang.

I was one of the lucky ones that night, I managed to actually get ashore. As he picked the telephone up he stood to attention and I knew from his posture that it was an Officer on the line. A Full Corporal came into the Guardroom and said to me, 'Are you going ashore son, cmon, I'll give you a lift.'

Deal really didn't have too much to offer but for those of us who managed to escape the net it was worthwhile. Just to stare at a pair of tits or a mini skirted leg. To sip at a pint of beer or to look into a shop window. Another good thing about the Services is that not only do the NCOs bawl and shout at you and the Officers look down upon you as if you are a piece of dog shit but they pay you as well. My first pay packet amounted to twelve pounds and ten shillings a whole ten quid more than when I was a joiner . . . Mr Brown, eat your fucking heart out.

On rare occasions they sometimes held discos in the camp and it was at one of these hops that I met my first true love. She was blond and petite and came from Sandwich which was very apt as I could have eaten her. She was gorgeous. I tried and tried to get my wicked way with her and then one day, the day before we passed out of training at Deal, she invited me to meet her mum. It was with great trepidation that I asked the Corporal for permission and when he said Yes I was running straight back to my grot for the Old Spice. We talked to her mum and Dad for a while and then we walked to the beach holding hands. Occasionally we would stop and I would kiss her softly on the lips as her little white dog yapped happily around our ankles. She had brought a transistor radio with her and as we walked slowly along the Stones and the Swinging Blue Jeans belted out their vibes for us. The sky was blue and there was not a cloud in sight as we lay on the sand. Presently, with my trousers around my ankles and having made sure there was no groups of young anglers about we made love. It was one of those desperate riving affairs when my toes dug into the sand to gain more purchase and as we both reached a stupendous climax, her dog started to lick my arse.

We would frequent a place called the Dive Bar in Deal, but when I look back we would go with the Flo. Flo was a lovely girl and although I never actually gave her one, most of the lads did. One Sunday afternoon I was out and about around Deal when I noticed a pier where some guys were fishing. The old tingle was still there and as I watched my mind cast back to the Heugh and those long summer days back home.

'Put a lugworm on the hook,' said a young lad to his mate.

'What the fuck's a lugworm?' replied his pal.

On reflection, those days spent at Deal were without doubt some of the best days of my life. We were map reading one day, perched on top of some white cliffs whilst high above the seagulls soared. I could picture in my mind's eye all of the young pilots who had soared above these same cliffs during the war years. I thought about Port Clarence and just what I had escaped from and how my life had changed. I thought of the years ahead of my life as a Royal Marine Commando and I thought of home and to be truthful, I didn't miss it. 'Just keep your head down,' were my dad's last words as he left me at Middlesbrough Railway Station all those months ago. I had thought about him as a young lad too and how the Imperial Japanese Navy had torpedoed HMS *Repulse* during the war and left him floundering in shark infested waters. How he had seen his mates torn to pieces by the voracious sharks only yards from him. I thought too about my Uncle Eddy who my Mam had told me so much about and who had been shot dead in his parachute as he floated down over Arnhem. What would the world hold for me?

Gan

Situated about 600 miles south-west of Sri Lanka lie the tropical Maldive Islands surrounded by the sparkling Indian Ocean. During the early war years a fuelling anchorage for ships of the Royal Navy was established at Addu Atoll the most southerly of these islands. 500 men of the 1st Royal Marine Coast Regiment landed on these islands and by December 1941 had established a base with coastal defences and roads being built by hacking through the jungle. The most southerly of these islands was established as an air base and remained so until the total withdrawal of British Forces during the early 1970s. For over thirty years the natives of Gan relied entirely on the British Forces for their welfare and livelihood and then it stopped . . .

CHAPTER 3

Commando Training Centre Royal Marines

'From the shores of old Antarctica
Where the Yanks have never been,
Lies the body of a fucking great Polar Bear
Fucked to death by a Royal Marine' ANON

When we arrived at the Commando Training Centre I must admit to being a little bit nervous. I think maybe that what I have just said would be a bit of an understatement really. I was shitting myself.

'As I was walking through the wood,
I shit myself I knew I would,
I cried for help but no one came
And so I shit myself again' ANON

We had heard all the stories about the place. About the gravestones set in the grass along the roadside. About the Tarzan course and the scramble course and the lack of intercourse. We had piled off the train and somehow managed to march up the hill whilst trying to carry every bit of kit that we possessed.

'FORM UP IN THREE RANKS!' shouted the Corporal, as we neared the camp gates. There was a drummer there, to drum us in, as we stumbled and cursed at the equipment that we kept dropping. We tried to march but it was impossible. As we entered the camp we noticed, or rather felt, a feeling of impending doom and as I recall, a window opened along the way and a lone voice said 'You'll be sorry.'

Actually it wasn't as ball breaking as I thought it would be. Granted there was the physical side of things that left you knackered but at least here the Instructors were actually instructing and not telling. We had passed the major part of our training at Deal and now we were within a few months of finishing training and joining a Commando Unit. Shore leave was very pleasant around Exmouth and Exeter and there was an abundance of pretty girls to choose from. We were told from the first day that we joined. 'Outside the gates, there are girls waiting for you. Any of you. They want to marry you. They want to fuck you. They want Royal Marines. They will do anything to trap you.' Sounded fucking great to me and I must admit to having my fair share or to 'Filling my boots.' Apart from Saturday mornings when we had the usual slog of the endurance course, the weekends we had to ourselves. I used to sit around the quayside in Exmouth with a pint in one hand and a fanny in the other. I would watch the fishing boats come in and feel envious as the punters climbed the quayside laden with fish. I longed to be out there with them pulling in pollack and cod or those huge conger eels that I had heard so much about.

I remember lying under the stars on the beach one night feeling very contented with five pints of scrumpy inside me and a wench bucking up and down on top of me. I felt rather whimsical and light headed as we made our way back to the nearest pub. 'A pint of scrumpy please landlord,' I said, 'and a blackcurrant top.' As he walked away to pour my order I noticed several old codgers nudging and winking at each other as they played dominoes. As my girlfriend turned around I noticed that the hem of her dress was caught up in her knickers and her chubby stockinged clad legs and suspenders were in full view. There was sand still sticking to her knickers but who was I to spoil the old codgers' fun. We had another three drinks before we left that place.

Towards the end of the training there comes the Commando Course and this is when the hard work starts. You have been built up for this over months and months of physical training and this course is the accumulation of all that hard work. The speed marches and the endurance course were absolute ball breakers but I only really struggled with the six mile speed march. I had been on the piss the night before in the NAAFI but after that I learned my lesson. I still passed that particular event but it was a struggle. Eventually it was passing out day and all the mams and dads came down to see us. All except mine. The Adjutant gave me my Green Beret and I must admit now that I cried my eyes out, not that I let anyone see, you understand. I had come a long way, a very long way and I had achieved so much through my own efforts. Even my shit stood to attention when it plopped into the pot.

Having passed out of training you could then specialise and through the old sweats in the NAAFI I had learned that the Heavy Weapons branch was the cushy number so I dutifully applied for the course and passed it with flying colours. The next step was postings. Where the fuck do we go now? Well I went in to see the Officer concerned and he explained the situation. 41 Commando are in Malta, 40 and 42 in Singapore with 3rd Commando Brigade HQ and there's 45 in Aden. Now fuck Aden I thought, there's shooting going on over there, the last place I wanted was Aden.

'Well it's like this, Sir,' I said, wringing my hands. 'My dad was sunk off Malaya in HMS *Repulse* you see and I would love to see the wreck. Apparently at certain tides you can still see it Sir, and, well I would love to see it, Sir.'

I got a posting to 42 Commando in Singapore and when I got there I thought I was in paradise. But there were a few things to clear up in Exmouth before we left. Now one of my old pals who shall remain nameless but his number was Bywater, had never bothered with girls at all, mainly because he had a cracking girl friend at home. He couldn't drink either which was a bit of a shame. However, seeing as this was to be our last night in England he decided to come ashore with us to fill his boots. We had done the rounds of the pubs and my girlfriend Liz had brought her younger sister Judd along with her for the night and he had plied her with plenty of drink. Now those Exmouth girls could drink but poor old nameless Stewart couldn't. We ended up back at the girls' house and we had a pleasant chat with the parents who as I remember were very friendly toward us. Presently dad said, 'Well, we'll be off to bed then,' And away they went . . . Well.

Now as I told you he couldn't drink and he had had about seven pints of rough scrumpy. I was on the settee giving it big licks and I noticed from the corner of my eye that Stewart was sat to attention obviously very shy. The girls excused themselves, after a whispered discussion with my bit, and I leapt over to Stewart and told him what to do.

'Just put your arms around her and look deep into her eyes Stew, and then stick the lips on her.'

'I'm shy but,' he said.

'Go on son,' I said, 'You can do it.' When the girls came back I winked at Judd and she winked back, in on the plan now you see. She sat down, Stewart put his arm around her shoulder, looked deep into her eyes and then spewed all over her.

We walked back into the camp that night at about three o'clock in the morning. We were pissed as farts and neither of us had filled our boots but who gave a fuck. Tomorrow we were off to Singapore, the world was our oyster . . .

'I looked at the stars where an elephant's eye

Was looking at me through a bubble gum tree' . . .

We were still 17 years old.

We sang our little cocks off that night as we walked through the camp.

'STOP THAT FUCKING RACKET!' (shouted the duty sergeant . . .

'FAAAARK OFF!' I shouted back.

The next morning at 5.30 a.m. we were in the galley peeling spuds, peeling cabbage and peeling turnip. Stewart developed a terrific sore on his hand and when we eventually arrived in Singapore he had to be interned into hospital for a week to sort it out. We were escorted out of the camp the very next day and held at Exeter St David's Railway Station until the train arrived.

'Do not darken these hallowed halls again,' said the Provost Sergeant as the train departed.

We arrived at Heathrow rather the worse for wear having sampled a few beverages in the local hostelries along the way. The flight wasn't due for an hour or two so we booked in and went into the departure lounge bar and sampled a few more. After a quick recce around the duty free I opted for a bottle of rum as I had heard that this was what all those fucking big hard Marines drank. We boarded the plane, a four prop charabanc, and I was as shocked when they told us to run like fuck to get the bastard off the ground. We drank steadily throughout the flight and our first port of call was Istanbul. When we alighted, the heat hit us and I had never experienced anything like it in my life. For someone who only a few months ago had never been to Whitby, Istanbul was a culture shock.

As we set foot in the arrivals lounge awaiting the plane to be topped up with two stroke I noticed that all the locals were on their knees and were bowing to someone. 'Fuck me,' I shouted gleefully, 'they want to play.' At that I proceeded to try to get them to play leap frog. I was in the lead and I was leaping over one and then the next. 'Away lads,' I shouted 'Fucking join in.'

'Hands up,' he said. 'Fucking hands up Abdul.'

I said, 'Do you know who I fucking am' . . .

'Hands up' said the Constable as he pulled the bolt back on his .303 Lee Enfield rifle. I was arrested and to be honest I was extremely disgusted with myself because if I hadn't have been pissed I could have filled all twenty of them in. They kept me in a room until the plane had refuelled then wheeled me back on a stretcher sound asleep when the plane was due to take off. They left me on the plane at Bombay and when I eventually awoke one of those lovely Stewardesses came along and said, 'Are you alright now?' Can you imagine those circumstances. You have just woken up from a slumber deeper than death and when you awake, there in front of you is an angel. Her eyes were light blue and the lipstick on those accommodating lips was deep red. Her hair was blonde and the sun shone through the windowlight and cast a halo around her head. I said the first thing that came into my head, 'Any chance of a blow job?'

She never talked to me all the way to Gan, our next destination. However we arrived at Gan which was an RAF Base and alighted onto the tarmac.

'Where's the fucking bar,' I enquired, as hard as fuck, and one of the ground crew pointed me in the right direction. Now believe this or believe it not, I couldn't give a shit either way but the lad that told me this swears that it was right. In the arrivals lounge at Gan they had a parrot. Now seeing as this was an RAF base the lads used to use the bars when there was no planes due and the parrot used to get constant attention. They used to teach it proper English vocabulary and the word 'Fuck off' was prominent in this. So when a 'Kite' arrived all the married bits and the kids used to talk to this parrot see. 'Hello Polly,' they used to say. 'Fuck off,' said the parrot. Now this came to the attention of the Commanding Officer of Gan air station at the time and he said, 'Well fack me, your ladyship,' after a complaint had been registered. 'I will sort this facker out.' Which he duly did. 'You will have to let the facker go,' he said.

The lads were gutted but orders was orders and so it came to that sad and sorry day, when they had to let the parrot go.

'Polly,' said its owner, 'It is with great regret that we let you go now, please don't think that this has anything to do with me,' and then he opened the doors of the cage.

To anyone who has ever been to Gan, you may know that there are some birds around the island called Skite Hawks, commonly known as shite hawks. Now these birds will eat anything and I mean anything. They will take the sandwich from your hand as you eat it and they will attack any other bird to kill and devour it. As Polly's cage opened that day, and she flew off, fluttering her feathers that had been constrained for many years, her wings hardly opened and as she struggled to make height, the shite hawks swooped. When last they saw Polly, she was being pursued out to sea, being chased by three shite hawks and shouting, 'Fuck off, . . . Fuck off.'

CHAPTER 4

Singapore

The Jewel of the East it's called. 'Some fucking gemstone this,' I said as we stepped out of the charabanc and onto the hot simmering tarmac of Payer Lebur airport. It was like getting kicked in the face with a pair of sewer man's waders. The smell and the heat was unbearable. For anyone not having the experience of going to the Far East it is hard to explain.

Anyway, we had arrived and after the grilling at the customs desk . . .

'What this mean on Passport, Government Service' . . .

'It means that I am a servant of her Majesty's Government' . . .

'What that mean, Her Majesty' . . .

The four ton wagon arrived and we chucked our gear inside. We travelled through villages or kampongs as they are known and this was so unlike Port Clarence. Still plenty of poverty about you understand but a different kind of poverty. There were stalls at the side of the roads everywhere, selling every mortal thing that you could think of. There was hundreds of black Mercedes taxis driving about and the drivers all seemed to be honking the car horns at once. Dressed as we were in UK clothing the sweat dripped from us when the vehicle stopped and when we reached the camp we were pissy wet. Having done the joining routine the Sergeant Major gave us the rest of the day off, to acclimatise, and so we jumped into a taxi and went out on the town. Singapore is such a fantastic place with so many cultures living alongside each other.

The driver dropped us off somewhere in town and we walked and walked for hours taking it all in. The taxi drivers kept stopping and saying, 'You want girl, John,' 'You want blue movie, John' 'What you want, I get John' and they were right. You could shag a donkey in Singapore if you so wanted, there is something for everybody. Anyway, we took up one of the taxi drivers' offers and he took the four of us through the town honking his horn at everybody as he went.

We pulled up outside a particular house and there sat on the porch was the biggest most beautiful girl that I had ever set eyes on. She was about six foot tall weighed about twelve stone and she was gorgeous. She was Eurasian which meant that she came from mixed race parents and as she sat there on a sun lounger, we stared at her and the world stopped. Slowly she opened her legs as she stared back, revealing a pair of frilly white panties. The taxi door slammed and as we stared with utmost astonishment, Gerry an Irish lad, who was one of our mates walked forward and reached out and took her hand and led her inside. We just sat there, as seventeen year old lads do, with our mouths wide open and about three minutes later Jerry came back. There was steam coming from his head and the smile on his face said it all. 'Boi fuck, that was brilliant,' he said. 'Fuck it' he said, 'I'm going back for some more,' and he did.

It was hard at first to acclimatise to the heat and the powers that be knew this and so for the first few weeks they made us take it easy. The Unit was away to cover the pull out of British Forces from Aden and everything was great for a while. Eventually the Unit came back and when we saw those Marines, so brown, so hard looking I think that we were just a little bit scared.

'Are you coming ashore tonight?' said one old sweat. 'I haven't got any money left,' I said.

'I didn't ask if you had any money,' he said, 'Are you coming ashore?' and that's the way it was. You were a team player and everyone looked after each other.

The friends that I made in the Royal Marines will be friends until the day I die. You were part of one great big family. OK you had your off days the same as everyone does but when you are expecting your mate to watch your back on active service you had to trust him. I could write a book about Singapore and everything that we got up to but I can't here. So I will condense it and tell some of the stories that stick out.

Two Geordie Marines in a brothel in Singapore. The bouncer paraded the girls and having chosen one each they sloped off to the cubicles near by. Now George, who finished before Geordie, was sat outside drinking a bottle of Anchor beer. 'Howay, young un,' he said. 'Haven't yee done yet.'

'I won't be long son, get the beer in.' So George ordered the beer and drank it. 'Howay, young un man,' said George 'Get a move on.'

'Why, hould on a minute man,' said Geordie, 'I didn't rush you like, did I' . . . so George ordered another bottle of Anchor and drank that as well.

'Now fuck this,' thought George 'I'll gan an see what he's up to.' As he peered over the wall of the cubicle he saw Geordie, clad in a rubber Mac with a Sou Wester on his head. He was wanking like fuck and the girl was flicking his knackers with an elastic band . . . True story.

Two Yankee Marines on leave from Vietnam.

'What do we do Hiram,' said Rocky, 'We put all the tables together see, and then we take a running jump along the tables, hit the parapet and then dive as far out as you can and land in the swimming pool two floors below.'

'Jees, you Guys are something else,' said Hiram as he stripped to his shorts. 'What's the bet?'

'One hundred dollars.'

'What, one hundred Singapore dollars, or one hundred dollars American.'

'One hundred dollars American Hiram, if that's OK.'

'Sure guys,' he said, as he prepared to take his run up. 'The American Marines can whip the arse off of the British Marines any day.'

Hiram took his run up. He thundered along the floor and hit the tables. He picked up speed as he approached the parapet. He hit the parapet at about three hundred miles an hour and dived out forming the perfect swallow dive. No one had told him that they had emptied the pool at six o'clock . . . True story.

Nobby Beck in the Paris Bar in Nee Soon talking to some Aussie soldiers. Of Polish descent was Nobby and the conversation went something like this.

'Fans, dey always av fans in da ceiling don't day.'

'What, are you cold or summat like a big daft, Sheila.'

'I stop da fans.'

'And how do you propose to do that, Limey' said the Aussie Trooper.

Nobby stood up, climbed onto the table in front of him and stuck his bald head straight into the fan. The fan stopped dead in its tracks and then Nobby dived off the table and landed on his head with a sickening crunch. He then picked himself up and sat back down at the table and said, 'Your round OZZIE' . . . True story.

The Jungle

Pitch black at five o'clock in the evening, the jungle is an awesome place. It is full of great big creepy crawlies, the likes of which you only see on those David Attenborough wild life programmes. During the day it is a hot sweaty mess of creepers and vines, ants and leeches. It is so hard to explain and the Tarzan movies that you see on the TV do no justice to it all. We had been yomping for hours and the shoulder straps from the webbing equipment had rubbed and chafed the skin from around our shoulders and hips. We were absolutely done in as I remember, suddenly, the lead scout stopped and started to sniff the air. There was a pungent odour the likes of which I had never smelt before and the word was passed down the line . . . Tiger.

We moved slowly on, not daring to look left or right just in case we stared straight into the eyes of this giant pussycat. Suddenly, as quickly as before, the lead scout stopped again and once again started to sniff the air. This time there was a stench of something rotten which we swiftly discovered was emitting from the half eaten carcass of a wild boar. You don't get many of those in Hartlepool. We had to stop for the night fairly soon as the day was quickly turning into evening and that's how I spent my first night in the jungle. Every little sound, every little noise when you can't see anything at all sent shivers of fear down my back. I never slept at all that night.

But as with most things you got used to it, you had to. Being covered in leeches and surrounded by buzzing hordes of biting mosquitoes came as second nature after a while but one thing that we learned quickly is the need to never become complacent. The jungle can bite and it does with venom. On one particular occasion, we stepped from the bush onto an old logging track and as we did so the heavens opened up with such a deluge. Now having been yomping for hours in the steamy heat a nice cold shower wouldn't go amiss and so we just stood there and let the rain wash away the stink from us. The track quickly filled up with rivulets of water as the monsoon pounded all around us. One of the patrol screamed and fell to the ground clutching his thigh. As we ran to his aid, a centipede about a foot in length appeared from the bottom of his trousers. It had been washed down the track with the rain and had managed to climb onto his jungle boot and then shot straight up his leg. It stung him so badly that in seconds his thigh was swollen so much that we had to cut the trousers from his leg. He survived but the lesson to us all was not missed as we watched the departing chopper.

Part of our jungle survival kit was home made and consisted of as many things as you could get into an old tobacco tin. Fish hooks, wire for snares, matches wrapped in polythene, razor blades, glucose tablets and that sort of thing. Now having bivvied up early one night and being close to a stream I decided to go for a butchers and low and behold there was some small fish topping here and there. I quickly assembled a rod from a piece of bamboo and made up the rest of my tackle from the contents of my survival pack. Baiting the hook with wood lice I was soon into some fish and I was quite enjoying myself until I noticed a bigger swirl beneath the water. A head appeared. The unmistakable head of the biggest fattest snake that I have ever seen. My departure was altogether very undignified and I even left the fish that I had caught . . .

You must, in the jungle, keep in constant radio contact with everyone else around you. Other patrols, Headquarters, safety etc. It stands to reason that if something untoward did happen, you needed assistance as quickly as was humanly possible and so at night a vigilant radio watch is kept.

As the earphones crackled one dark night, a little voice came up on the radio and said, 'WHOOZAT' . . .

Several seconds later another voice came up and said 'WHOOZAT WHO'S SAYING WHOOZAT' . . .

Several seconds later another voice came up and said, 'WHOOZAT WHO'S SAYING WHOOZAT WHO'S SAYING WHOOZAT' . . .

Several seconds later another voice came up and said, 'WHOOZAT WHO'S SAYING WHOOZAT WHO'S SAYING WHOOZAT WHO'S SAYING WHOOZAT' . . . and then HE came on the air.

Talking with a mouth full of marbles. 'Hello all stations, this is zero, whoever that is who is mucking aboyt on the radio, I must inform you that you are breaking proper radio procedure and it must stop at once. If it doesn't, I will find oyt who it is and I will have your guts for garters.

Several seconds later a little voice came back 'WHOOZAT' . . .

But Singapore wasn't all about the jungle. It was about enjoying everything that the place had to offer and of course one day I discovered the fishing. They were man made rectangular holes, dug into the ground with mechanical diggers, filled with water and topped up with carp and other exotic species. I came upon the first pool by chance having got lost on some map reading exercise and the following weekend I returned with a couple of mates. You could hire six foot solid glass rods that were an improvement on my gear back home. Bait would be supplied in the form of bread paste and you could enjoy a pleasant afternoon catching small Grass Carp and Java, a perch like fish that bristled with indignation when you hooked them.

Arriving one Saturday morning, I found that the lake was full and that every peg had been taken. I discovered that the RAF chappies had also sussed out this little corner of paradise and that they were firmly embroiled in a fishing match, the likes of which I had never heard about. The year was 1968 and the banter around the lake was about the fishing in England and some up and coming young angler called Ivan Marks who was plundering the sweep money. Some of these lads had brought along fishing magazines sent from England and I was enthralled to be reading about the exploits of Ivan and the Likely Lads.

Now this is where my old sparring partner Barry Clapp came onto the scene as he had just arrived from Blighty. Barry, as I, was fascinated in the match fishing game so we decided to give it a go. We bought all the latest ABU equipment and tackle to go with it. We sussed out a wonder bait and fairly soon Barry was winning every match. What was this wonder bait – corn. But just not any old corn you understand. First we would go the local market and purchase a ten kilo bag of what we called pigeon corn. Now having been involved with pigeons at an early age, this gave us a bit of an advantage you see as we had a good idea of how to prepare the stuff properly. We would boil it for hours in a dirty big pan and then let it cool off whilst we had a couple of cans of Tiger beer. The next procedure and this was the killer, was to leave it then for about six weeks until it stunk. The smell was revolting and the aroma stayed on your hands for weeks after you had used it but it certainly worked.

I have read recently in the angling magazines about the smells that linger on your hands, like cigarette smoke and petrol. But I think that it goes beyond that. I think that certain individuals give off a certain smell that fish seem to find off-putting. I have that smell about me and Barry hasn't. We would use identical gear with identical baits and Barry would catch ten carp and I would catch one. We would change rods and he would rebait and catch straight away whilst I wouldn't have a bite on his gear. Anyway, the fun that we had with this type of fishing was tremendous and those balmy days so long ago seem like a dream now. Barry went on to become a very good match angler with Catch Match who won a National along the way but he has left fishing now to concentrate on breeding pedigree dogs.

Sea Fishing Singapore

We had heard about a long jetty that the RAF used from time to time and so one day we decided to give it a go. Stocking up on essential supplies like Tiger beer and white harbour ragworm we set out to conquer this jetty. Having paid off the taxi driver who had honked his horn for the duration of the ten mile journey, we set foot onto the jetty which stuck out into the South China Sea for about a quarter of a mile. As we neared the end of the jetty we noticed that we were not alone and that we would be sharing our platform with about six Chinese gentlemen who bowed and smiled at us as we arrived.

'We'll show this lot a thing or two,' we thought as we tackled the ABU Beachcasters up. Using the pendulum swing we cast out and as the terminal tackle sped out seawards, I shouted, 'Look out Hitler, that bastard's going to land in Germany.'

We never had a nibble. Not a crab, not a fish, nowt. The Chinese gentlemen hauled up sand shark and bream like fish on their handlines. Fish after fish after fish. We slunk off with our tails between our legs and stopped half way along the jetty well out of earshot as the Chinese gentlemen giggled and chatted. We couldn't go home yet though as we still had nearly a full case of Tiger beer to get through so we impaled a couple of white ragworm onto the hooks and cast out. As we sat there talking about old times back in the North East we knew then just how lucky we were to be there. Two little raggy arses sitting having a beer under a tropical moon . . . marvellous.

'Did your rod top rattle then, Tone,' said Barry.

'Crabs man' I answered, but I gave the rod a good yucking just in case. There was something big on the end and it was fighting back. Eventually I brought in the ugliest looking catfish. It had barnacles on it and corns and warts. It had whiskers and it was ugly. It was so ugly that I felt disgusted and booted it right in its head. No one told me that they had poisoned spikes on their sides. Well, the Doctor did when he cut the trainer from my grossly swollen foot. As Gary Pucket and the Union Gap belted out 'Young Girl' we would be sitting around a swimming pool watching all the fillies go prancing by. The Vietnam war was raging and thousands of people were dying as the B52 bombers dropped their deadly payloads daily onto that poor embittered country not so very far away from Singapore and guys of similar ages to ourselves, of similar backgrounds were being slaughtered in the name of peace.

CHAPTER 5

Going Home

I flew home from sunny Singapore and landed at Brize Norton without so much as a whimper. It was summer 1969. The shock of seeing how much older people were and how my siblings had grown, far outweighed the first delicious taste of a bottle of Double Maxim. My brothers were talking in gruff voices and doing dot to dot on each other at night when the others were asleep. The shouts of anger echoed throughout the house the next morning when they found that someone had joined up all the zits on their faces with a felt tipped pen. I joined the old gang again for a couple of weeks whilst on leave and to my surprise they hadn't changed much. They still enjoyed the occasional forays to the Heugh but these days most of their spare time was spent in the hunt for an accommodating member of the opposite sex. We would often go to the Graythorpe working men's club near Hartlepool on a Saturday evening to enjoy the live music and if you pulled a bird it usually meant a long walk home from there. People couldn't afford taxis you see, so Shanks's pony was the mode of transport. Having said that, most of us usually caught the last bus home but I feel sure that all of us would have preferred the walk.

On one particular occasion, I had dressed in a lightweight brown suit that I had had made in a twenty four hour suit shop in Singapore. I wasn't on the last bus that night and as I set off on the long walk home I had grass stains on the knees of the trousers and the elbows of the jacket. As I stepped out with my chest puffed out and my shoulders swinging I started to sing,

'She wore, she wore, she wore a Globe and Laurel,
She wore a Globe and Laurel in the merry month of May,
And if you asked her why the fuck she wore it,
She wore it for a Bootneck who was far far away'
... and then, it started to rain. It came down very lightly at first and then there came a deluge that reminded me of the monsoon in Singapore. As I trudged through the storm, first one sleeve fell off my jacket and then the other. The next morning the trousers had shrunk and the turnups came almost to my knees.

I spent an unusual leave back in Port Clarence and at first I thought that the others had changed, until it dawned on me that it was I who had changed. I had just spent eighteen months on the other side of the world with fellow Marines whose attitude to life was so very, very different. I was glad to leave again, to return to the Commando Training Centre to forego a training course and then to get married ... I had met her in Singapore, she was fifteen, I was seventeen. It was a disaster from the start but let's not dwell on that. I passed the training course and then I applied to return to Singapore and was elated when my request was granted. So once again I set off on my travels and I narrated the story about the parrot to anyone who would listen when we arrived at Gan.

Years later I was shocked to read that when the RAF eventually pulled out of Gan they left a legacy of despair and poverty. Having relied upon the RAF for its economy, health and welfare since the Second World War the population of Gan had forgotten all the traditions of their forefathers in the fishing skills that they needed to survive. It's sad to reflect on the consequences that the British pulling out from the Far East had on these happy smiling people but I am sure that they survived. As the VC10 touched down on the hot tarmac of Payer Lebur Airport, I felt that now I was coming home. I was rejoining my adopted family in a place that I loved, only this time I had a young bride to look after as well as myself. The foliage of the jungle and the familiar smell and damp wet heat of the climate greeted me once again. So very unlike the bleak industrial outlook of that particular corner of North East England where I was born. There was no dense outpouring of choking smog from the ICI Chemical works at Billingham here. There were no declining ship yards and the vast unemployment that this would bring to thousands of hard working lads who joined their colleagues from the also declining Steel Industry into the dole queues.

Some of the faces had changed when I arrived back but Barry Clapp was still there having been joined by his lovely blonde young wife from Hartlepool, Kathy. We soon settled into the swing of tropical life again and of course the fishing took on a whole new lease of life as we plundered those carp at Lim Kah Seng's pond. Lim was a smashing guy who used to serve us with his beautiful wife's fried rice dish on a bamboo leaf. He would produce cold bottles of Anchor beer for us with the condensation streaming down the side of the bottle. He would appear as if by magic when someone latched into the bigger carp and he would shout 'BEEEEEEEG ONE' across the pond. The only bugbear in this corner of paradise is that occasionally you had to leap aside when a coconut husk fell from the high trees way above us. Sad, wasn't it.

Apart from the usual exercises into the jungle, which were second nature now to us old sweats, life in Singapore the second time around was marvellous, a constant, never ending enjoyment of swimming pools and parties, of barbecues and booze ups that would shock the everyday gentleman in the street. The dance of the fiery arseholes when a newspaper was stuck up the crack of someone's arse and then lit with a match. 'Hold em down, you Zulu warrior, Hold em down, you Zulu chief,' we would sing at the top of our voices before putting the miserable sod out of his misery by throwing our pints of beer over him. The egg fights that we had in the Cameron Highlands at the top of Malaya where everyone was covered in slimy broken eggs. The nights out that we spent in the glittering neon lit Singapore Town where we used to start off with a few beers in the Britannia club, an all services club quite close to the Raffles Hotel. As we pulled up outside the club one balmy evening Barry said to Kathy, 'Watch that monsoon ditch love.'

'What monsoon diiiiiiiiitch,' she said as we plummeted down the six foot drop. Then we heard the sad news that all British Forces activities in the Far East were being drawn to an end.

The sadness that I felt when I heard this news devastated me. I didn't want to go back to England and I suppose that no one else did. Defence cuts meant that the Garrison in the Far East had to be scaled down drastically. A trip to Australia and exercises in Borneo didn't cheer us up one bit, we had to go home.

Before we could leave however the British Government decided to hold a massive exercise to evaluate the consequences of its defence policy in the Far East. They needed to know that having once left, we could return if necessary to support local forces at very short notice and so came exercise Bersatu Padu. The scale of this exercise is hard to imagine and it involved massive air lifts from the UK, of stores and personnel to support the ground troops already fighting an imaginary battle against Communists forces. It involved the deployment of the Commando Units and their supporting batteries of artillery and engineers. It involved the Gurkhas and the British Army and it involved the Singapore Army. I suppose that I am being unfair and just a little critical here when I mention the Singapore Army. The average soldier stood about five feet two inches tall and I have seen more meat on Lester Piggot's whip. They usually wore skin tight olive green uniforms that wouldn't look out of place on a catwalk and to a man they wore sun glasses. During the exercise they had to pit their wits against the Mortar Troop of 42 Commando with disastrous consequences.

Now if you can imagine, the British Army has had a presence in the jungles of the Far East since long before WW2 and the skills obtained in this very difficult theatre of war had been passed on to generations of soldiers for years. The plan was, you see, that the Marines would be the baddies and a Regiment of the infamous Singapore Army would be the goodies. The goodies searched for the baddies and the goodies couldn't find the baddies. They were given map references but they still couldn't find the baddies. So the exercise umpires came to the baddies and said, 'Look, they have been trying to find you for over a week now, could you send someone down onto the track to make a bit of noise and then let them follow you back up here, we can have the battle and it will be all over.'

So two Marines, Spike Press and Oggie Gelaghtly, went down onto the track and as the lead scouts passed, Spike and Oggie ran out onto the track and let rip with a twenty round magazine of 7.6mm blank and a belt of fifty rounds from the General Purpose Machine gun . . . The whole Regiment ran. It took the umpires over two hours to catch them all . . . Suddenly, it was all over.

After a big parade when the Units of all our combined battle group stood and cried as the Union Flat was lowered and a lone Royal Marine bugler played the last post, we only had days to go. We paid off our wonderful house servants and they left with tearful farewells. 'Don't go back England,' they cried. 'You stay master, you stay missy.'

We handed in all our Aussie lightweight equipment and our Armalite rifles, the canvas jungle boots and the bottles of mosquito repellent. We said our goodbyes to our Chinese neighbours and we had a farewell drink in the Raffles Hotel before we left. As the VC10 banked over the airport I had my last glimpse of Singapore far below. The foliage was as green as ever and the blue sea glistened and sparkled. I saw a tiny dot of water and hoped that it was the pond of Lim Kah Seng that I saw. I can still see Lim standing there now with a cold bottle of Anchor beer in his hand shouting 'BEEEEEEEG ONE' across that memorable lake where a young man from Teesside came of age.

CHAPTER 6

Plymouth 1971 to 1976

The aircraft was buffeted by high winds as we approached Brize Norton airport and the heavy clouds prevented us catching our first glimpse of England through the windows. We arrived and touched down safely and started to unload from the aircraft. Support Company 42 Commando was home and as we hurried to the arrivals lounge, babies and small children were crying. The single lads had sat at the rear of the aircraft and had enjoyed themselves so much swigging bottles of rum. The journey to Plymouth was uneventful apart from the noise from the still crying babies, especially our own pride and joy, our daughter, Patricia. We were housed initially in a big house just off Mutley Plain in Plymouth and we had three long months of leave to look forward to. Having settled in, it was then time to travel up to the North East again to visit the folks. However this time we would be visiting Darlington as my Dad had decided to go into the pub business and at that moment the family was residing in the Copper Beech in Neasham Road in the town.

An uneventful week or two and then we returned back to Plymouth for another house move, this time over to a shared house in Milehouse. I was watching the television one night when a knock came to the door. Clappy stood there laden with fishing gear and a daft look on his face. 'Can you put me up for a couple of days?' he said. As it turned out he had entered a three day boat fishing competition out of Plymouth and of course I said, 'What a fucking good idea.'

We quickly sped down to the Plymouth Sea Angling Centre and we both booked in and paid the sweeps. The next morning

46

there wasn't a cloud in the sky as we drew for which boat we would be on for the day. There was no wind and the blue waters of Plymouth Sound sparkled. A Royal Navy Frigate swept majestically out of the Sound as the smoking diesel engine of our little boat pounded furiously to keep us afloat.

'Did you hear that old codger on the quayside,' said a rather fat gent as he struggled to squeeze his ample proportions into an all in one wetsuit. 'He said that there was a big wind coming up from Cornwall.'

'Daft old sod.'

We stopped to feather for mackerel, our bait for the day and fairly soon we were butting out again into the ever increasing swell with the bait bins full. There was a pretty middle aged woman on board who I later found out was Rita Barrat who held a world record for a certain line class caught shark. The wind increased in its velocity and suddenly we were hit with the worst of it. By this time I was on the bottom of the boat talking to God. 'Oh God,' I said as the bile from my stomach came up time and time again. It must be the most nauseous feeling in the world being seasick and the worst thing is you can not get off. I wrapped an old tarp over my head to block out the mountainous seas around us and one time as I peered bleakly out from my hiding hole we were at the bottom of a trough. The giant waves were high above us and all I could see was a green wall of sea all around us. It was about this time that the tarp was ripped from me and the skipper shouted 'Quick, get this lifebelt on.'

As I struggled with the straps, I looked up and there stood Rita with a cup of tea in her hand. 'Poor lad,' she said as she looked down at me. The skipper had to turn the boat and head back in to more sheltered waters and he did this extremely complicated manoeuvre with the utmost skill and I am very sure that this man's seafaring aptitude saved our lives. Around the coastline when the wind hit us that day, a lot of people drowned on pleasure craft that were overturned by the gale force winds that battered the South West. I stuck it out for the following two days however, and achieved nothing in the way of prize money but at least I caught a fish or two, especially a near specimen garfish. That was my first trip afloat on a small boat and even though I suffered badly from sea sickness I was a regular angler heading out for the Eddystone reef most weekends. My companions never took sandwiches because they knew that they could eat mine. On one particular occasion when we were loading onto the *Boa Pescador*, one of the most famous of Plymouth's boats, a bobble hatted angler was just tying up his own small boat. Fitted with a powerful outboard engine, his boat could reach the reef in about forty minutes. He had been out to the reef by himself early that morning and as he tied up he showed us a sparkling bass of huge proportions. 'I've got a record here,' he said and he had.

The usual method of plundering the hordes of fish that lived on the reef was the red gill rubber sand eel, a stiff actioned boat rod and 30lb line attached to a fast multiplier, a weight sufficient to get your bait down quickly which was sometimes around a pound. Just above the lead weight we would attach a heavy brass swivel onto which we would tie on a 20 foot trace of 20lb line and then the rubber eel. The crack was that you lowered the lure quickly down to the bottom and then started to retrieve it in jerky movements. We would catch cod and pollack and whiting. We would catch bass and pouting and sometimes someone latched onto a conger eel. I vividly remember the first time that I came face to face with one of these denizens of the deep and the experience certainly cured me from my sea sickness that night. We had set off for an evening session, as I remember and all on board were Servicemen. We headed for the Hands Deep reef but on the way the steering cable on the boat snapped. 'You might as well drop your gear over the side,' said the skipper. 'This could be a long job.' The engines were cut and the boat drifted along with the swell. My stomach revolted as ever and even the dark sinister black shape of a Submarine slipping by couldn't detract from my feelings of utter hopelessness.

'Fuck me,' said Jan, a huge bloke with a full beard,' I've

latched onto something big here.' After an almighty struggle he boated a huge conger and as the skipper plonked it into the plastic fish bin that was housed in the centre of the boat it slid up the other side and as I looked up its huge cavernous mouth was about an inch and three quarters from my nose end. 'Shiiiiiit' I screamed as I climbed the mast with the dexterity of a blue arsed monkey. It took the lads for ever to stop laughing but I didn't come down from my lofty perch until I thought it was dead.

I remember being out on the reef one day when some shark boats were up from Looe and were drifting along with the tide. We could see someone ladling the rubby dubby from the rear of the boats which is a mixture of chopped up fish guts and pieces of whole fish. This revolting mess is a great attracter of sharks and one of the lads on our boat propped his rod against the gunwhale whilst he poured a cup of tea from a thermos as we watched the boats drift by. Two things wrong here: first, he had cast out away from the boat and instead of waiting for his lead to hit bottom he had just let it plummet down uncontrolled, the second was that he had baited his huge hook with a whole mackerel in the hope that a prowling conger would snap up this delicacy. His rod suddenly shook and then flipped over the side never to be seen again. It might have been snagged on the bottom but you know how these stories go. 'Shark,' said the unlucky angler whose eyes were bulging in his head and I think he believed it.

Another trip and another day of sea sickness for me but this time we were fishing out of Exmouth. As we boarded the boat that morning a gentleman in a fine worsted suit, white shirt and tie and polished brown shoes hailed us.

'I say, chappie,' he said to the skipper in a plummy accent. 'Do you mind awfully if I join you?'

'Not at all,' replied the skipper. 'But you'se hardly dressed for job, is you.'

'I don't mind,' he said as he stepped on board. 'Do you have any spare tackle?' . . .

We stopped to feather for bait fish and pretty soon the bait box was full of shimmering mackerel. Now Barry had managed to snag a dogfish on his feathers and he took it upon himself to show us all how to gut and skin this small shark. After a marvellous exhibition of flexible fingers, he skinned and gutted the fish, and soon he had a pile of guts and intestines in front of him. 'And that's how you do it,' he said, as he heaved the remnants over the side. Now as we were travelling into a facing wind, the guts and intestines were caught by the breeze and quickly whipped around and smacked the suit straight in the face. I've never laughed so much in all my life.

We had another guy on board that day who constantly took the piss out of me as I brought up my stomach. The mickey taking went on all day and it was beginning to wear a bit when suddenly Barry winked at me. He tapped my offender on the shoulder and as he turned with that mocking smile still on his face, Barry picked up a mackerel and bit its head clean off, right in front of his face. 'Huuuuuueeeeeey.'

But it wasn't all about boat fishing, far from it. There is a big sandy bay just a few miles from the Torpoint Ferry called Whitsand Bay and it was from here that we used to try to catch those big silver bass that prowled about the breaking surf. Not that we ever caught any you understand but it was a lovely setting to try your arm at beach fishing. With huge cliffs and tiny worn paths down to the beach, it reminded you of a smugglers' cove of old. You could just picture a one eyed, one legged pirate landing his boat in the surf, with the parrot perched on his shoulder, shouting, 'Pieces of eight, Pieces of eight' and Clappy standing there shouting, 'Ow pal, we're trying to fish here.'

There is a coastal path that runs for miles from Torpoint right along the beautiful rugged Cornish coastline and it was with great pleasure that I stepped out one night with a pack on my back and a fishing rod in my hand. As I remember it was August Bank Holiday and that Friday evening was one of those never to be forgotten evenings when the blackbirds sing constantly from the rooftops and high above the seagulls floated on invisible thermals. A slight warm breeze ruffled through my hair and in the distance I could hear an ice cream van chiming its come and buy one melody. Children were playing tag in the cobbled streets and the look of enjoyment on their faces as they dodged between the parked cars was a pleasure to behold.

As I approached the path I stopped for a while to light a cigarette and to adjust the straps on my pack. A cheeky grey squirrel chattered at me indignantly and then skipped away along a branch back to its nest. I walked for hours marvelling at the ruggedness of the place, the white surf pounding below and the green heather and bracken stretching far away until it reached the cultivated farm land. I would clamber down through the rocks when spotting a likely gully and flick out a spinner to try to capture my supper but really it didn't matter if I did or not. I would sit and just watch the movement of the waves and listen to the cries of the sea birds in this splendid isolation. As the twilight approached I lay down my sleeping bag just above the high water mark in an area clear of bracken and set about making my supper. As the pan bubbled on the stove, I felt that there was someone watching me but as I looked around I could not see anyone but the hairs on the back of my neck told me that I was being observed by someone or some thing. I picked the pan from the stove and the delicious aroma of tinned stew filled the air and then I noticed the vixen sat about twenty feet from me. We looked at each other for a while and then I sort of just carried on and she still sat there, just watching me with those big unconcerned brown eyes. I had brought some bread and I ripped a chunk off and threw it to the fox but she didn't move at all. I lit a cigarette and took a swig from the whisky bottle and then just as night set in, she disappeared as mysteriously as she had arrived. Throughout the night as I lay there in the open, looking at the stars, I listened to the sea and the soothing sounds of the breakers as they hit the beach close by, I thought about life and all the beauty that it can bring. I thought about times gone by when I had looked at these same stars in a different part of the world and I thought about a fox that had shared a moment in time with me ... Wonderful.

CHAPTER 7

Farewell to the Marines

The weeks turned into months and the months into years. We were constantly on the move and at times we would be sick when we found out that we were going to Malta or Gibraltar again. We were sick of drinking in Famagusta and Limasol. We were growing tired of constantly having to have our gear packed to depart at a moment's notice. We would vanish into the night and arrive back four months later. It was hard on the families and equally hard on us at times. My little girl was growing rapidly and I was missing it all. She was the life and soul of the playgroup but at times I felt that I was a stranger to her. When I came home she never recognised me and although I didn't show it, it hurt.

The Commando carriers *Bulwark*, *Albion* or *Hermes* were our homes from home and we travelled extensively throughout the world on these great ships. We would fly off the flight deck of the carriers, in waves of Wessex helicopters and it is a marvellous sight to be up there amongst a 'Stick' of choppers laden with fully armed Royal Marine Commandos going to do your stuff. The smell of the Avcat aviation fuel as the choppers flew close to the ground, would drift in through the open door and sometimes you would have to rope down if the terrain was unsuitable for a landing.

On one particular NATO exercise in Turkey, we landed without mishap and as we took up firing positions to cover the departing choppers I noticed that there were dozens of tortoises around us. We grouped up and set off yomping for the rest of the day and just before dusk we stopped for the night and bivvied up. After posting the sentries and setting up defensive positions for the night it was make your meal time and the other preparations necessary for a night's vigil. We had with us that night a Forward Observation Officer, a Captain of the Royal Artillery. Now, as he set up his position for the night, he rolled out his sleeping bag and this was too good an opportunity to miss. It didn't take us long to capture a tortoise and as someone caught the officer's attention, someone else slipped it into his sleeping bag. As darkness fell, we stood to just in case we were attacked and when the 'Stand Down' was ordered, he slipped tiredly into his sleeping bag. It took about five minutes before he found that he was sharing his bag with someone else and when he screamed we thought that we were being attacked. He ranted and raved and then produced a torch, the beam of which he quickly directed into his sleeping bag. He held his SMG at the ready which wouldn't have been much good really as the magazine was full of blanks and slowly the intruder appeared. As the hard shelled assailant sped away the Officer reshone his torch into the bag and said those immortal words, 'The bastard's shit all along me sleeping bag.'

Another bit of fun concerning one of these self same officers occurred on one of the Dutch West Indies Islands of Vieques. We had been yomping all day, as usual, and for some reason he was at the head of the patrol. Suddenly he came shooting back along the column shouting, 'Tarantulas, Tarantulas!'

'Will someone please go and catch that officer,' said the Company Commander as we went off to investigate.

Sure enough, spread across a gap between some trees was a huge web, and there perched with their eight legged menace sat five huge Tarantulas. Having caught the Officer we boxed around the nest of spiders and carried on yomping until dusk. Now what we didn't know was that this poor Officer had a real bad manic phobia about spiders. Anyway, we selected high ground for our night position that night and went through the well known regular procedure. Sad as it was, our hero plonked his sleeping bag right under the only tree on the hill and on this tree was one leaf. He blew up his air bed and then his air pillow and then smoothed out his sleeping bag. He then gave his orders to his assembled party and slipped quietly into bed. My companion and I were slightly lower than him on the hill and when the leaf fell and floated slowly through the air and landed gently on his nose we could see everything. As the leaf touched his nose he leaped from his sleeping bag screaming, 'Tarantulas Tarantulas!' It took us about five minutes before we regained our composure and our jaws were aching with the uncontrolled laughter. As we approached him, he was standing on his blown up bed holding his trousers up and he was delirious.

'KILL IT! KILL IT!' he screamed.

'Just hold on there,' said Frank 'I'll find it for you' . . . and that was when Frank saw the leaf. 'Oh yes, Sir,' he said quietly 'There it is, just beside your big toe.'

It was a terrible thing to do to an Officer of Artillery. The Officer screamed and shouted hysterically and sobbed his poor little heart out. We never laughed so hard, or for so long, ever again.

Another event that same evening which made it a night to remember was that a fighting patrol being led by a Geordie Corporal of Marines was going out as Frank and I were just about controlling our laughter. You know what it's like when you have these bouts of laughter and then you stop and then you think about it again and then you start to laugh again. Well we burst out laughing just as the patrol passed us and as we were lower down the hill the Corporal couldn't see us.

'Wee the fuck's that like?' he said as he stopped. The rest of the patrol piled into him and he shouted, 'Ow man, divn't get too close or you'll be up me arse like.'

Frank and I laughed for hours. We laughed so much that we cried and when we pictured that Officer doing a dance on his sleeping bag we laughed again.

In between those months of sailing the seas, we would spend brief periods at home and try to capture some quality time with our families and then we would be gone again. We would always try to get in a bit of fishing somewhere along the coast but these brief interludes were few and far between. My wife and I were growing more distant after every trip but at least my little girl still called me Dad. She showed me drawings and paintings and chatted incessantly about her friends and it hurt to leave her again when the time came.

On board the carriers, although they carried nearly two thousand men, it could still be a lonely place and if you needed to be by yourself for a while you could always find a quiet spot amongst the Bofors platforms or the Seacat spacings. It was there, on the Bofors platform one night that I sat and read the 'Dear John'. Although expected, it shook me to my roots when I read it. I was miles out to sea and there was absolutely nothing I could do about it. As I sat and watched the waves roll by in the gloomy twilight, I read the letter again and again and then lit a cigarette. Somewhere out there in the Mediterranean Sea there is a gold wedding ring. When I look back, I can't blame her for what happened. I was enjoying post marital sex in every place that we landed. I was, all in all, a stranger to her, coming back as I did from my jaunts around the world, uncaring, unloving and demanding. I drank in excess and smoked too much and the arguments and the things that we said to each other hurt deeply but there was one person that was hurt more, as she listened to it all from her bedroom, my daughter Patricia.

Much the same story had happened to Clappy but the reasons for his marriage break up included a memorable event that should go down in the annals of history. The wives, as they do, had a wives club and on the day in question Kathy was entertaining. Our hero returned home from the camp much the worse for wear with his beret on the back of his head and singing his head off. We had said our farewells that day to a colleague who was departing the Corps and the resulting booze up was a pearler. 'Don't mind me, lasses,' said Clappy as he plonked himself down into a chair and promptly fell asleep. The Colonel's lady and the other Officers' ladies and the other ladies just carried on with their stiff British upper lips and continued to sip their cups of tea and nibble away on their biscuits. That was until Clappy stood up, lobbed his todger out and pissed all over the floor ...

I decided to buy myself out to make a go of my marriage but even that didn't work out. One day my little girl said to me, 'Is Ray coming around today, Dad?' as she referred to my wife's sailor boyfriend who had spent three months living with her. After a few months in Colchester I returned home, a dejected down hearted soul with a broken marriage and a broken career behind me. My family were by now living in Yarm in the Ketton Ox and I settled down to try to collect myself together and to gain some sort of normal life. I managed to secure a few jobs but it was very hard to settle down having been on the move constantly for the past ten years. That was until one day when out walking the dog I spotted someone fishing and catching roach after roach and big silver dace.

CHAPTER 8

Yarm 1976 to 1979

Purchasing the correct tackle wasn't the problem it was how to use it that bugged me. I could watch for hours, the youngsters and their Dads swinging in clonking big dace from the 'Free' stretch at Yarm, but when I tried it, it seemed that nothing went right. Who said I still can't fish. I'm sure that I just heard someone casting doubts about my angling prowess. Probably right anyway...

But anyway, along the grapevine I heard that there was an angling club in Yarm so I set forth to find it, after all, where better to learn your trade than in the company of brilliant anglers who I was sure would be prepared to pass on some secrets. Wrong ... I am still waiting for the secrets to be passed on to me. I duly joined the club and lo and behold I found out that they held fishing matches and it was with great expectations that I sallied forth into my first proper match.

Frank Flynn was match secretary then and as I walked up he said, 'NAME.'

'Now where have I heard that before,' I thought. Anyway I paid my sweeps and as I was looking at my ticket with peg 22 on it I heard someone say, 'There's Dave Harris over there, he won a National you know.'

'What the fuck's a National,' I thought at the time. But it would be many years hence that I actually found out.

Having been told how to get to my peg I couldn't wait to get there and when I did arrive I was heavy with sweat. The River Tees was tidal then and in front of me the water was very low and gin clear. The sun was shining and it was pleasantly warm as I pulled my ABU beachcaster from its bag. 'This'll hold 'em,' I thought, as I attached the multiplier full to the brim with 30lb line onto the rod. I filled the size 1/O Aberdeen hook with about twelve maggots and sat back waiting for my first bite.

Yes I know, it's hard to imagine but I did struggle that day and in fact all I caught was one small dace. Hard to believe, isn't it and that's what the scaleman said to me when I weighed it in. 'You're not weighing that in are you?' he laughed. Now I must admit that I was a little bit annoyed until he said, 'Here son, follow me.'

A few pegs up from me on peg 27 there was an old chap who explained that he had only a few bits to weigh in and then when he pulled his net out of the water, he duly weighed in 29lb of chub, dace and big golden roach. I was amazed, absolutely one hundred per cent amazed. I had never seen anything like this ever and from that moment on I was hooked on match fishing. I thought at the time that I would soon be weighing in catches like that and do you know, I am still trying. But I loved it. The camaraderie, the leg pulling and the hoping that one day, one day, I would win a match with a catch like that. I always remember those words that Mick Grainge said to me all those years so. 'Don't go in the sweeps son.' I wish I had taken his advice because it must have cost me thousands of pounds over the years. I was well into match fishing then, but one day a familiar face popped up and for the next six weeks I caught more fish than anybody has ever caught at match fishing at Yarm.

'Hello Barry,' I said, as I noticed his little blonde head amongst the beer glasses in the Ketton Ox.

'Now then ugly,' he said. 'I've got a job for you.' Now this news was music to my ears as I was a little bit skint but when he said 'We're going to work on my brother's trawler out of Hartlepool,' I nearly shit myself.

'A BLOODY TRAWLER, A TINY JUMPED UP, NEVER COME DOWN TRAWLER'. . .

'Shut up you big Jessie,' he said, 'And get the beer in.'

So we travelled to Seaton Carew and set up shop and of course seeing as we wouldn't be going out until four o'clock the next morning we set out to drink all the beer in Seaton. 'She wore she wore, she wore a globe and Laurel' Oh we sang our little hearts out that night as we staggered home with arms around each others shoulders. Barry's mum had prepared supper for us and we soon got stuck into the half chicken each, the roast potatoes and the mountains of vegetables. The hot gravy was dripping from the plates when she served us and she whispered softly to us, 'STOP THAT BASTARD SINGING'. As I lay my head on the pillow someone tapped me lightly on the arm and said 'GET UP YOU LAZY LITTLE TWAT.'

It was freezing outside that morning. One of those miserable hoar frosts that covered everyone's cars and made the going underfoot treacherous. We boarded the boat and cast off and as I looked at my watch it told me that it was 3.45 a.m. As we rounded the Heugh breakwater the chicken came up, then the roast spuds and then the veg. I wedged myself into a bunk and fell into a deep sleep that was disturbed by the sounds of motors and engines running. When I climbed unsteadily onto the deck the lads were preparing to shoot the net and as I walked forward to lend a hand, Terry, Barry's brother, told me to get out of the way as this was one of the most dangerous operations on board a trawler especially as the boat was rolling and tossing with the swell. I noticed that it was still pitch black and so I decided to get back into my bed. I must admit that I heard the net being drawn back in but I thought sod it, let them get on with it.

'Tony,' said a voice very very quietly. 'Tony, wake up.'

I opened my eyes and at first thought that my eyes hadn't adjusted to the gloom. As I peered at my surroundings I noticed that lying along my arm was the biggest lobster that I had ever seen. It had whiskers and feelers and all sorts of things protruding from it and the biggest pair of pincers on the end of its arms and these pincers were waving about just under my nose.

'YOU BASTARD!' I screamed at Clappy as he rolled along the

cabin floor killing himself with laughter. That was my initiation into the trawler business and for the next six weeks I was the butt of all jokes. Like the time Clappy farted as he stood on the stairway that dropped down to the cabin. It was one of those really smelly farts and he barricaded the stairway so that I couldn't get out. With my stomach, and the rolling and pitching of the boat and that smelly fart there was only one conclusion . . .

When the net was swung in and the cod end was opened the fish would fill the decks. We would stand knee deep in fish, every sea fish imaginable, and then we had to gut them. This was a horrible cold job in the freezing weather and your fingers and hands were blue with the cold. The gutting knives were razor sharp and one slip could result in a nasty gash if you weren't careful. As the gates of the net disappeared into the dark water we knew that we had four hours until it came back up again so everything had to be done as quickly as possible. We would sort the fish out by species and then the prawns by size. We would stack them and ice them and drop them into the hold, and then the net would come up again. It was knackering work, freezing conditions combined with the tossing and pitching of the boat. Barry said one day, 'Would you like a flat in Hartlepool?' When I answered to the affirmative, he gave me a flounder. . .

We would arrive back into the harbour and unload the fish. It would be about nine o'clock at night and then we would go for a few dozen pints in the same clothes that we had worn all day. We always seemed to get a seat in the local pubs and I must admit that the people of Hartlepool are very generous in this respect to strangers. One dark miserable morning as we left the quay, Terry tapped me on the shoulder and said, 'Did you hear what I said?' To be truthful, I hadn't heard one word, and to make things worse, I still couldn't hear him.

What had happened you see, is that the constant pitching and rolling of the boat, it had effected my equilibrium and I had gone deaf. Completely and utterly mutton . . . It was eerie, it was frightening and of course being made to work in one of the toughest environments on earth, with a bloke who can't hear, well it just wasn't on was it. So we had the day off. We loaded black bags with fish and prawns and crabs and set off to Yarm where we would sell our wares and get enough money for a night out. The bus conductor gave us some very funny looks as we boarded but when we presented him with a big slab of cod for his supper he became very friendly towards us, especially when he started to have a sip or two of the bottle of whisky that we produced.

'Hey, ladsh,' he said, 'Lovely bit of haddock that ish, I'll have it for me shupper tonight.' As we stepped from the bus laden with umpteen black bags reeking of fish he was singing his head off. 'Thersh an old Mill, by the shtreeeeeem, shmelly dean.'

It was good to be back in Yarm and our first port of call was the Ketton Ox.

'Do you want any fish, Mam,' I said to my good lady and that little knowing smile at the corner of her mouth said it all.

'Do you want a pint, lads,' she said. So many years had passed since last I had brought home a bagful of fish for my Mam.

The six weeks on that trawler did me the power of good and it brought home to me just what people would do for a living to provide food and clothing for their families. A hard life, a very hard life and one that I am glad not to do. It is with deep respect that I now raise my glass to trawler men wherever they are and wish them luck.

Suddenly it was Christmas and thank goodness Barry had departed back to British West Hartlepool and left me alone for a while. The Ketton Ox was decorated throughout with the trimmings and the decorations and the tree. The family were gathering for the festive season and it was the intention that we all spend it together this year. We bunked the little kids in drawers and the big kids on the floor. We scared the hell out of them with tales of the Ketton Ox ghost and then we grown ups joined in the festivities. When we awoke, all with bad heads, I said to one of my brothers, 'Fancy a bit of fishing, son?' So presently, when the girls had got their act together and their warpaint on, we set off in Ian's battered old Marina and headed for our favourite bait digging place in the whole world. We stopped at the Royal in Port Clarence for one and renewed some old friendships and then set forth to dig some of those big fat lugworm and ragworm. As we arrived the tide was just backing up and the snow was falling lightly around us. We struggled to walk through the initial black stinking oozing mud but thought no more about it as we set to with the garden forks. We soon had plenty of worm for bait and just before we stopped digging, I thought, 'Oh, that looks like a good place' so I started to dig again.

The place that I had selected to dig was in the deeper, more oozy stretch of mud and as we were pulling out those big fat ragworm I hadn't noticed that I was sinking deeper and deeper into the mire. I tried and tried to extricate myself but as I struggled I only sunk deeper and deeper. I tried to pull my feet from the Wimpey logoed wellies but I couldn't, I was well and truly stuck. The tide was well on its way now and the gullies were rapidly filling with freezing water as the estuary flooded. The steam was rushing from my head as I pulled and pulled and stretched to get out of my predicament but to no avail. I could see the concern etched on my brother's face as he tried everything to get me out.

'Hold on Tone,' he said, 'I'll go and see if I can find some driftwood or something to help me get you out.'

He plodded away through the mud in the gloom and he left me with a smile on his face. A worried smile and then I knew that I was in a serious condition here. I was starting to get cold, very cold and the snow fell around us with those big soft flakes that cover everything. The water was creeping slowly toward me and we were about a mile and a half from the nearest road. I couldn't see Ian through the snow now and I lay on the mud with my legs and waist enclosed in the black stinking mire.

'She wore, she wore, she wore a globe and laurel, I sang quietly to myself as the fingers of icy cold water stretched toward me. Suddenly Ian was in front of me. 'Give us a fag, son,' I said. I didn't notice that he had been dragging an enormous piece of driftwood with him and that he was completely done in. He collapsed onto the mud and at first he couldn't talk, he was so tired. He had dragged this piece of wood for about two hundred yards through the black oozing mud and the exertion of his physical effort had left him completely knackered. 'Get ... get onto the wood,' he said. 'Quick' ...

The tide was unabating and it was now lapping around my midriff. I couldn't feel the lower half of my body, it was so cold. I stretched out and grabbed onto the wood and managed to get a good grip even with my frozen hands.

'PULL!' shouted Ian as he tugged on my jacket. 'Come on you big daft twat, get out ... get out.' He had tears in his eyes as he looked at me and I knew then that I was going to die if I didn't get out.

I prayed. 'Help me, God' I shouted as I struggled with my tiredness and the cold. The numbness in my lower body was a serious concern now but suddenly I started slowly to drag myself onto the driftwood. The muscles in my upper body responded as I pulled and pulled and with Ian's help I managed to pull myself from death.

But the ordeal still wasn't over. We still had to negotiate several hundreds of yards of black stinking mud that was by now filling with the ever increasing tide. We splashed through the icy cold water oblivious to our surroundings and we couldn't even see the shoreline through the now heavy falling snow. In what seemed like an age we reached the shore and with only one pair of wellies between us we still had to get to the road.

'Keep going, Tone,' said Ian, 'We'll make it.'

By now I was in the first stage of hypothermia and as he carried me on his back he was shouting at me. 'SING TONE, COME ON SING' ...

'When Irish eyes are smiling, sure there all as pissed as farts,' I sang and I sang and then we reached the car. Ian revved up the engine and put the heater on full blast and that glorious heat came bounding through the pipes and my lower body responded to it. I got severe pins and needles and then an enormous pain as the warmth swept through me. We passed through Haverton Hill and then through the ICI complex at Portrack, which was still belching out its noxious fumes, and then onto Yarm.

As we stepped from the car a group of beautiful young girls clad in the very shortest of skirts walked by with the obvious intent of having a good night out in Yarm. Their hair was made up wonderfully and the war paint that they wore on their white faces was stark, yet sexually very arousing. We were covered in mud from head to toe and the black mud stank of everything nautical. They giggled as they passed us, eyeing us nervously and as they walked away, with their hips swaying and their long bare legs stepping out, their perfume drifted toward me, I was so glad to be alive.

The match fishing continued for the next three years and on occasions Clappy would come over from Hartlepool and we would spend an afternoon catching those big dace and roach. After one of these sessions and just as the town hall clock was striking six we negotiated through the cars parked on the cobbled high street and went into the George and Dragon for a couple of pints. Now this was the age of the punk rocker and low and behold when we entered the George there were about six of them sat there. They were being extremely verbal and obnoxious and the landlady Pat looked a little bit concerned.

'Don't worry Pat, I'll sort them out,' Barry said. He popped outside to where we had left the fishing gear and popped a couple of maggots into a match box. When he re-entered the pub, he picked his pint up and went and sat right in the middle of the punk rockers. Their conversation stopped immediately as firstly they looked at Barry and then at each other in bemusement. 'Now then lads,' said Barry, 'We're going to have a little race see.' He produced the maggots from the matchbox a red one and a white one. He then dipped his finger into the beer of the biggest punk rocker and drew a wet line across the table. 'Right then, here goes,' he said and as the punks continued to look amazed the maggots started to wriggle towards the other end of the table.

'Come on the red one,' shouted Barry, 'Come on my son' . . . The white maggot won the race and as Barry picked up the vanquished red maggot he said, 'Useless bastard' and then popped it into his mouth and ate it.

HUUUEEEEEY. The punks jumped up and ran for the toilet with vomit dripping from their fingers as they tried to stem the flow. 'GET OUT, GET OUT!' screamed Pat as she threw us both out of the pub . . . Some people have no respect.

It was time to move on though and the wanderlust had returned to me. I needed to get away and one of the saddest moments of my life had just occurred. My Mam had died in North Tees Hospital after a long illness and I couldn't stay around any more. I needed to be back amongst my family in Plymouth once again. I hadn't been able to settle in Yarm, I was still, deep down underneath, missing the action and the comradeship. The craziness and the discipline of the Royal Marines just couldn't be resurrected here and I had been in trouble with the law twice for fighting misdemeanours, it was time to go.

CHAPTER 9

The Wilderness Years 1979 to 1982

For the next three years I had a variety jobs which included taxi driving in London, bartending in Ruislip and Strood and bouncing in the night clubs of Plymouth. But first I had to make my escape from Yarm. Things hadn't worked out between my latest flame and me and I had taken a shine to another girl who was just setting off to work in Strood. She asked if I could drive her car down and this I duly did. I stayed with her for a while, sneaking into her hotel room at night, but we drifted apart and I then managed to secure a job as a taxi driver. Being a quick learner I soon found out that if I talked in a southern accent I would get more fares so I would usually pull into the railway station at say Wembley and start ... 'Cam on then, me old shiner, op in' ... 'Where you gowing then Gav' ... And the other usual nonsense. After six months of ferrying people araaand Landan I was stopped one night by a posse of peelers from Hendon Police College. They asked me to blow into a bag the result of which was positive and I spent the night with the old Bill. It was time to move again but it is worth mentioning here that whilst working around this neck of the woods I met Chris and Kevin Finnegan, two boxers whom I have always had a great admiration for. I also attended a christening where Brian Whatsit (sorry I've forgotten your name) who was lead singer with the glamour pop group The Sweet was putting a few away too.

I arrived back in Plymouth with fifty quid in my pocket, a small suitcase and one pair of shoes which were very tight. I spent the night in the Crown, as it was then known, with one of my old muckers, George Bold. As we supped our pints and talked about old times it seemed that I hadn't been away. The money ran out after a day or two on the piss and my feet were in a sorry state with blisters appearing on top of old blisters. I went into the local DHSS and told them that I had nowhere to go and then propped my feet onto the counter to show the young lady. I was at my lowest ebb at that moment in time, lower than I had ever been before. She gave me a voucher to get a meal and another voucher to buy a pair of shoes and finally a voucher to stay in a certain hostel. I arrived at the hostel and a little Irish lady opened the door and said to me, 'You don't belong here, son.'

The whole building stank of vomit and urine. There were alcoholics sleeping it off, lying on the floor in pools of sick.

'You'll stay in here,' said the landlady as she led me into a room that was lit with a single low wattage light bulb. Lying in one of the beds were two drunks who still had all their clothes on. In another bed lay a cropped haired pasty faced man who I later learned had just come out of Exeter jail having just served a four year sentence for attempted rape. The bed that I was to sleep in, had an old pissed through mattress on it and a rough old Army blanket for warmth. I went to what served as a bathroom and the floor was an inch deep with water in which dog ends and used toilet paper was floating. I washed my face from the cold tap and tried to scrape the stubble from my chin. The wash basin was cracked and stained and there was a sort of grimy tide mark around it and there was blood caked around the taps.

I left the building feeling a little bit refreshed at least and walked slowly up to the Hoe and sat in one of the little shelters there and looked out over the sea. There were small yachts scurrying about inside the breakwater and I saw a fishing boat heading out probably bound for the Hands Deep reef for an evening session. I sat there for a long time and sobbed my heart out. The sun had gone down hours ago as I made my way back to the hostel. The night revellers buzzed happily around the town and took no notice of the shambling figure as he walked passed them. In the hostel I found that the drunks had gone through my suitcase and certain things were missing. I broke up a fight where one of the assailants was knifed in the stomach. I hardly slept that night with the continual biting of the fleas and the need to be constantly aware in case of an attack from one of the fighters who I had nutted to stop him from causing further damage with the knife . . .

I was rescued from my predicament by a guy called Dave Laurie, an old colleague, who took me under his wing and for the next two weeks I lived in Stonehouse Barracks where Dave was still serving. He managed to secure for me a job as a bouncer in the old Cascade club, a haunt for serving Marines and attached ranks. I felt that I was back home at this stage but my life lacked something and the girls who provided me with their undoubted charm and hospitality helped me through a very difficult period of my life. I have deliberately left out the six tours of Northern Ireland in my narration but for those of you out there who have been in the province you alone will understand why I did so. The bombings and the deaths, the massacres of all those poor innocent people, the friends who were hurt physically and mentally and the scars that still remain to this day. It affected us all, everyone who ever served out there. I don't think for one minute that the mental trauma that we sustained will ever leave us.

I had heard little about my daughter Patricia throughout these years but I always carried a picture of her wherever I went. I still have it to this day and I am happy to relate that we did meet again years later and her story was a very sad one and I feel that somewhere along the line I was to blame. My family back home was in the throes of marriages and divorces and the every day process of life was still rolling on. The bouncing game is a very hard life and eventually I succumbed to a seventeen stone nutter who knocked ten bells of shit out of me and at that stage I felt that once again the wanderlust had taken hold of me and I had to go back home. I was 32 years of age, very experienced in the ways of the world, I had been everywhere, done it all and had all the tee-shirts.

Before I left Plymouth, I had my last walk along the Hoe and the thoughts that went through my mind made me feel so sad. I had had a fantastic life so far, meeting some wonderful people along the way. People who I could rely on to save my life if it was needed. People who had loved me even if only for a short time and people who I will never forget.

Like Swain, a tall gangly Marine who I shared many a memorable time with. Dave and Jan Mitchell who brought me back into the land of the living. I visited this lovely couple just after Dave Laurie had found me wandering the streets picking up fag ends. 'Get them clothes off now,' said Jan. 'You stink.' So I stripped to my skiddies and she just stood there and said 'Them as well' . . . She washed and ironed my clothes and threw away my socks and skiddies whilst Mitch and I got pissed. It's hard to believe that Dave is now diabetic and his health isn't what it used to be. Buster Brown whose toilet I spewed over the second time that I served in Singapore and who also bounced on the doors in Plymouth. We had some hell of a good times together. Phil Hicks and his lovely lady wife Rita. Phil stopped a bullet in his leg in Northern Ireland and Buster rattles with bits of shrapnel. I think I'll weigh him in for scrap when he goes.

These were people, real people who I had shared some good times with and it was with great sadness that I boarded the train and headed back to the North East. But time moves on. I couldn't live like this anymore. I needed to find something that was out there, but I didn't quite know what it was. I had been back to my roots so to speak, to try to capture what I used to have, what I believed in, what I had enjoyed so much for ten years. Throughout the hardships and the good times, the memories still linger, of blokes that you would battle with one minute and defend the next minute. Of people who would rip your ear off and then send you a card in hospital and a bunch of daffodils to the missus to say sorry. Of Royal Marines who spent their youth being at the forefront of British troubles throughout the world whilst others paraded around the globe protesting against the Vietnam War, the war down the pub last weekend and the war against drugs. They wore flowered caftans and bunches of flowers around their skinny shoulders and they walked around shouting 'Peace, brother, Peace'. The only peace we knew was when they stopped their Jane Fonda similar speeches and kept their mouths shut.

CHAPTER 10

Back Home 1982 to 1997

I quickly renewed my membership of Yarm Angling Association when I arrived back and pretty soon I was back onto the match fishing scene. I will always remember my first trip to the River Trent where I caught fish after fish all day long. They were bleak and I must have had over 300 of these little bars of silver to weigh in 4lb 10oz. The river was in its heyday then and we used to travel to those big matches at least once a month. I remember catching 4lb of fish again in one particular match and this young chap called Dick Clegg, now England's manager, was the section scalesman.

'As tha got art?' he said as he walked toward me.

'About 4lb,' I answered.

'Tha's got abart two parnd more than me then,' he said.

Dick will never remember me, but what a moment that was to savour. I still recite the story when I've had a few. Fishing the Trent meant that we would be rubbing shoulders with some of the great household names like Jan Porter and Frank Barlow and I suppose that in some ways we became quite blasé about it. Frank came up to Yarm to present the annual awards just about a year before he died and I hope that Mo and Frank had a good time with us. We certainly did. Just to have him in the clubhouse meant that the prize giving evening would be a sell out, that was the attraction of the man.

I joined the teams who were competing in the various local leagues and during these years Yarm won just about everything that there was on offer. Something like winning the North East Winter League 18 times out of 20 speaks volumes for the class of angler who used to fish for Yarm. A split in the ranks caused by one of my pet hates, whinging, led this great team to disband and to go their own ways. Division one material in the Nationals, semi finalists and finalists in the Winter League. Winners of the Teesside league for many years it speaks for itself. We used to travel all over the country chasing those elusive big money prizes whilst on our own door step just under the surface was and still is one of the best match fishing rivers in the country. All it needed was a little bit of organisation and some hard work with the bank clearing tools and it would be revealed.

I had remarried now and my lovely young wife Lynda had given birth to our daughter Kathryn. We had our own house in Yarm and I could still get out fishing on a Sunday to compete against those lads who I still compete against although not as much as I would like to these days. Then came two periods of unemployment which is a non occupational hazard in the North East for anyone who isn't trained or who hasn't got a trade. I would still fish matches and use up vital money that we could ill afford to use and many times I left Lynda crying through my arrogance and stupidity. I remember fishing a March Open once at Yarm where all I had was the two pounds necessary to actually enter the match. The river was in flood and I was drawn along Rudds bank where I managed to find a slack into which a lot of little fish had gathered to shelter from the spate. I caught loads of them and weighed in about 2lb and came second. Ken Golightly won the match with a single chub and took the main sweeps. I won ten quid for a section win . . . Such is my luck. If I didn't have bad luck I would have no luck at all.

One dark horrible evening, Mike I'anson who was Captain of one of the Teesside League teams, stopped by and asked if I could fish the next day in the final of the knockout cup. The snow was falling and was blowing about in flurries and it was bitterly cold. 'Mike,' I said. 'I have no money, no bait and no transport.'

Mike answered in no uncertain terms, 'I'll pay your sweeps, I'll give you some bait and I'll pick you up in the morning.' That was the team spirit at Yarm in those days.

He duly picked me up and we headed for Hemlington Lake in Middlesbrough, the venue for the knockout cup final. A JCB had been operating at the far end of the lake and the water was a horrible chocolate colour as we started. The wind blew coldly over our heads and I fished a small block end feeder that day into which I had placed only six pinkies. No one was catching and in fact no one had a bite that day except me. It was hard to distinguish between the wind blowing the tip or actual bites but a slight movement emphasised by my target board had my heart racing. I reeled in and sure enough the end of the pinkie had been nibbled and so casting out again I gave that tip my whole attention. A slight movement again and I struck gently and felt the weight of something tugging back at the other end. I netted a small 4oz skimmer bream much to the mirth of the other anglers around me, but that fish won the match and the knockout cup for Yarm that year 1986. Mike never asked for his two pound sweep money back.

The previous year I had won a match at Yarm with one single roach of 8oz beating Steve Cooper who caught about eight tiny dace. The river that day was stinking of diesel because someone had tipped in a forty five gallon drum of it just up on Lambs Stream. When you cast in the bait was tainted straight away so the only way that I could fish was to place my baited hook into the palm of my hand and punch my fist through the water and throw the end tackle as far as I could. It worked, one bite one fish. The massive Hargreaves pollution had wrecked the River Tees and wiped out just about every living thing in its wake, small fish, big fish and plant life, crustaceans and microscopic plankton, everything. It was heart breaking to see. Large eels were seen trying to climb out of the River at Yarm whilst the gulls and cormorants feasted on this glut. The river was ruined but that marvellous organisation the ACA secured a massive amount of compensation for us all to the tune of £750,000. This money was used wisely and it is only now in 2000 that we are seeing the benefits of it. The river has for the past few years been slowly opening like an oyster to reveal just how well this money was managed. Match fishing and pleasure fishing alike has come on in leaps and bounds and the Tees Barrage has helped enormously to provide once again a marvellous picturesque fishery. We just stay ever vigilant to the continuing threat of pollution however because if it happens again on the scale of the Hargreaves disaster it will take another fifteen years to get it back to what it is now.

The National Championships was a competition that most aspiring match anglers just had to have a go at, but the way the system works is that just one team from any one club could compete. So when you have a club of 500 members it is very hard to actually break into the squad let alone the team and if you like me are just another average club angler it was impossible. So what do you do, you get off your fat arse and organise another team. For those of you who have competed at the Nationals you will understand why we all do it but first of all there was the actual joining system to navigate. Now seeing as we had no idea of how to go about it, I first of all contacted the National Federation Of Anglers. We saved all our pennies for the joining fees and eventually we went to a meeting in the East Midlands region over which that old stalwart and mine of information Gerald Rollinson presided. If it wasn't for this man's influence and knowledge of the NFA system we would never have got in but it's thanks to Gerald that we did. Sadly Gerald died some years ago and I never had the chance to thank this man for his efforts. Something that I still feel sorry about. Anyway, we were in and then we had to transfer to the North East Region which we duly did but this entailed more meetings, more pennies and then we had to get the team ... Fifteen months later we were ready to tackle the National Championships.

CHAPTER 11

The National Championships

'Where the fuck's the Forty Foot drains?' said someone. 'Is it forty foot wide or forty foot deep?' asked someone else.

'It's in Norfick isn't it?' said someone else.

'Well I've heard it's full of bream,' said someone else . . .

Meetings, don't they just get up your nose? Well they do me but there again, I've only been to crap meetings. They do say that some meetings are beneficial to a team but our lot had meetings to decide on what we discussed at the previous meetings because we couldn't remember because we was all pissed see . . . Some preparation eh. Anyway, we went down for a little practice and one of the lads picked up a fourth place in a practice match due to a foul hooked Zander and we thought that we had it sussed and we were on our way. Wrong. We had secured a sponsorship deal through a local business man and the proud logo of Cleveland Stresstest was emblazoned across our Halkon Hunt Jackets as we all met at the HQ that Saturday morning. As I looked around at our motley crew I realised that something was wrong but just couldn't put my finger on it. I was to find out later, at the end of the match, but firstly I had to get my priorities right and find a toilet. Now for those of you who have never attended a sit in on match day it goes like this. Your stomach is still full of warm beer that you had somehow imbibed about a gallon of the night before. Probably the curry or the kebab is sloshing about as well and as you stand there in the queue the old crimper is twitching furiously. You smile at the lad in front as the queue goes slowly down and then you smile at the lad behind you when it's your turn. The seat is still

76

warm as you whip the old trollies down and just when you are about to let go, you remember the queue outside . . . Some of the competitors creep into the ladies toilets for a dump but do you know, I couldn't face Sandra Halkon Hunt if I had just been into the trap and she was next . . . well could you?

We drew a crap peg and the heat beat down on us as we set off on the official coaches to our pegs. It was the hottest day of the year and as we travelled slowly to our section the sweat dripped from my forehead as I read the write up from *Angling Times*. Suddenly the coach conked out and we just sat there, cast adrift in the middle of the boondocks sweating our cobblers off.

'It's broken down,' said the driver. An observation that at that moment in time was just what we needed. He started to try to get it going but to no avail and eventually a returning coach rescued us from our peril. We arrived at our pegs at 10.45 and as I struggled with my gear I said to one of the stewards, 'Ow pal, where's this peg?' I was one of the lucky ones that day and my peg was only a short run away from the parking spot. I arrived at my peg at 10.50 out of breath and as I dropped my gear I noticed that the far bank had some lily pads attached to it and that there was some little fish topping off them. 'Waggler,' I said as I stripped off my shirt and started quickly to assemble the rod. The heat was murderous and reminded me of those years ago when I had fished in similar conditions in Singapore. As time was shouted I was just about ready and I flicked the 2AAA waggler across the lily pads. I had no time to put in any bait but as the float settled it slowly sunk and I struck into a small roach which I quickly kissed as I dropped it into the keepnet. My first National fish and I was on my way.

Throughout that day the maggots died with heat stroke and the pinkies curled up their tails and did likewise. The only bait to survive was some gozzers that one of the lads had given to me. I had time to rig up a bomb rod and lost a big eel on it that fell to smelly lobworm but at the weigh in I had succeeded in amassing 96 points (I think) out of 104. Not a bad effort but the team had fared somewhat differently. Four blanks meant that we wouldn't win anything but we did have one guy, Ray Brown. who took section money and came about thirteenth overall which was brilliant for him. Back at the HQ I learned that we had come about sixtieth and one of the lads said, 'Well, it's not bad for a first go.' I was gutted. I was used to winning team events I couldn't take that shit and then someone told me that there had been a fracas in the pub the night before. I was boiling at the time, not because of the heat but because of a combination of things that had led us to let ourselves down and my dreams of a National win were shattered.

I've fished five Nationals since and have never come in the first sixty yet so my anger was well misplaced and out of order. The following year we were on the middle Trent, a river that we all knew fairly well and one that we were supposed to do well on. As a river fishing club we went there with the expectations of at least promotion, but oh how wrong you can be! I drew an area at Hoveringham that hadn't produced a fish since Pontius was a pilot and as I set up the silt came up to my knees.

'Tha won't catch nart art o' there,' said a local wag as he wandered by. At about 10.50, just before the all in, a flock of about 100 geese floated serenely down the river towards my peg, cackling and laughing at these daft humans.

'Ow George,' said one of them. 'Look at that dickhead over there standing up to his knees in the silt, doesn't he look pissed off.'

'Shall we give him something to be more pissed off about?' said his mate.

'Howay then,' and they just started a fight. 100 geese having a battle right in front of you and you are there to get as many points as you can ... Gutted. I tried everything that day. Wag and mag, feeder and bomb, stick float and whip and then I just sat on my box and cast the bomb in again with two little pinkies wiggling about on a size 24 hook. AT 2.55 I caught my one and only fish. A roach of 8oz that managed to get me 46 points out of 80. Is it worth it? Of course it is. One day, maybe one day, someone, some young angler will say to his mate 'There's Tony Curnow over there, he won a National you know.'

CHAPTER 12

Club Fishing

Throughout these years there is something that I still feel quite proud of and something that I never want to let go of. Club fishing is what it is all about for me anyway. As a young lad all those years ago the friendship and the camaraderie of fishing as a group, generated a feeling of belonging to something and something that even now after all these years is still with me. Coach trips to the Trent with groups of anglers who were more interested in the day out than actually catching a few. We sometimes had good anglers who would frequent these matches with the full intent of plundering the sweeps but the sweeps were kept low to discourage this type of angler.

I remember one particular match when I had stood at Yarm Town Hall freezing in the cold whilst waiting for the Head Wrightson's club coach to pick me up. I had waited for over an hour and then as it pulled up and the lads loaded my gear into the boot I staggered onto the coach to face one of the lads who said, 'Fuck me, Tone, you look nithered, here get some of this down ya.' Gratefully expecting a hot coffee that might just get some warmth back into me I sipped at the warm brew and the look of shock on my face had everyone on the coach that day laughing. It wasn't the expected coffee but tandooried pigeon ... It was delicious. We would arrive at the Trent and having drawn for the peg numbers we would set off. There would be little tommy cookers going all day warming up soup or coffee and then the whisky bottle would come around. Sometimes we would catch a few and then again sometimes we wouldn't but it didn't matter you see, you were fishing.

The Tioxide club were another club who loved the Trent and it was a pleasure to fish with these guys. I well remember coming second to former Barnsley Black John Smiles with 12lb 2 oz and John beat me by 2oz. I remember going there and blanking but mainly I remember the good times that we all had. Sadly these coach trips are now a thing of the past but the memories as always, will stay. Thanks. At Yarm we had a good club match fishing scene with a good junior section and thirty or forty of us would compete for the club trophies each year.

I remember fishing one particular match when the river was still tidal and I had drawn in a good area at peg 23 on the shallows. I had fished the waggler across to a near side glide and had been catching well and was holding my own with the eventual winner Gez Byrne who was on peg 22. As the tide turned I had to move further and further back until I was right back up the bank and right under a tree. It was impossible to fish anything but a straight lead down the side right under my feet because of the foliage above my head and for the rest of the match caught only a few very small dace. If I had been able to continue to use the waggler, I would have caught a lot more and some years later when I became Match Secretary of Yarm it was something that I put right. If you fish anywhere and you pay sweep money, I feel that you should be able to fish any method that you can throughout the match and no matter who you are, you should be able to compete and catch fish with any method at your disposal.

The characters that I have met over the years through fishing have always had the same thing in common and that is the sport. It brings together people from all walks of life and at Yarm we are no different to any other club in the country. The laughs that these people generate are talked about for ages after every match when the beer is flowing and the crack is at its best. Geoff Keech, a well known angler on the North East match circuit and a very good angler, is one of these characters. Arriving late one morning for a match with bleary red eyes he told everyone that he had been stuck in a traffic accident after

81

an articulated lorry had thrown its load of wigs. He said that as he left the scene the police were combing the area ... Peter Jackson having been snapped by chub time after time on the Harkers Farm stretch was told by Geoff Gray to put some heavier line onto his reel. 'Fuck off,' said Peter, 'I've still got 2000 yards of this 2lb stuff to get through yet.'

At another particular match at Cod Beck, a tributary of the Swale, Peter cast out into the heavy fog and eventually he had a bite which he quickly struck at and managed to snag a chub. As he reeled in, the chub went up the tree and as he back wound it went back down again. He had cast out over an overhanging branch due to the fog and the chub was led a merry chase until he managed to net it ... There are many, many characters who make up every club membership and it is without doubt that they contribute so much to the day.

CHAPTER 12

Focus on Yarm

Throughout these years back home I felt eventually that at last the wanderlust was slowly passing out of me and that I was settling down but events led me to having to pack the old war bag again due to work and although the Channel Tunnel project meant big money and a comfortable life style, it also meant being away from home again. Away from my family and away from the fishing but all wasn't as bad as it seemed. It was hard to be split up from everything that I now had but the sight of the lake at Allhallows Holiday Park on the Isle of Grain, Kent, just kept a little smile on my face. Situated on the peninsula between the Thames and the Medway this holiday park hosted caravans and chalets and was an ideal spot for accommodation being as it was only a few miles from the Isle of Grain precast yard. For nearly three years, I clicked on and off at this arse hole of the world but I couldn't pack it in as the money was so good.

Anyway, we found this holiday complex and rented a chalet and then I transported some of my fishing gear down to the place. The lake held a fair amount of common carp, ghost carp and mirror carp. It also held a sizable head of lovely marked rudd the likes of which I had never seen before. Clocking off at 7 p.m. each night meant that there usually wasn't sufficient time to have a good go at the fish but the weekends proved different. We used to finish work at 3.30 and then rush back to the digs excitedly and run down to the lake. Most of the locals were into boilie fishing for the carp and they would set up their bivvies and their buzzers and pile the boilies in and then sit back to wait for bites. Having found a swim vacant one day next to two of the bivvie brigade, I set up and rigged for carp as quickly as I could. In about thirty minutes I had four carp and two fat tench to my credit, much to the chagrin of the bivvie boys who hadn't managed a run all day.

'Wot yo using then mate?' asked the angler next to me whose head was covering with one of those Dick Walker hats.

Well, it's a mixture of unbleached flour, yeast, soya flour, salt, vegetable fat vinegar and emulsifiers,' I answered as I read the ingredients from off the bread packet.

'A new recipe is it then, mate,' he answered back jealously as he copied the ingredients down.

'Oh I pal, it's a Northern recipe that is,' I answered as I struck at another carp who had taken a fancy to my piece of bread.

The rudd in the lake could be caught by using a small crystal waggler with no weight down the line and a size 20 hook onto which you impaled floating caster or floating maggot. I had been catching a few of these beautiful fish one summer's evening and as darkness descended I noticed another one of the bivvie boys fishing alone who was latched onto one of the ghost carp.

'Nice fish, pal,' I said as he slid his net under it.

'What a beautiful end to a wonderful day,' he said. As I looked at him I thought, what a prat ... he must have been watching too many of those John Wilson videos and as the sun dropped below the horizon I sort of just came out with it ... FAAAAARK ORF.

Every third weekend we would travel back up the A1 and arrive back at around midnight or 1 o'clock in the morning. Saturdays used to be spent recovering from the tedious journey and Sundays used to be spent with preparations to go back down to Kent again. Sometimes if we were having a long weekend at home I would fish a Yarm club match on the Sunday morning but I was as sick as a Redcar donkey on a Bank Holiday Monday when I had to go back. Team fishing was still going on whilst I was away and sometimes I would still get picked to fish in the Teesside League Championship match at

Burton Joyce, Nottingham on the River Trent, annually. This sometimes caused a few problems especially when the car that I was travelling in at one time broke down and we spent the night under the stars in some garage along the A1 until being rescued by the AA. I arrived home at 5.30 had some breakfast and then the guys were there to pick me up to travel back down to the Trent.

On another tiring weekend when the same thing happened we were due to fish in a Regional match on the Leeds Liverpool canal. Pole fishing was the order of the day with bloodworm and joker as bait for the mainline and caster and hemp for the far bank. We also took along liquidised bread to use with the bread punch, lob worm and those small red worms that you find in manure heaps. Pole fishing was just starting to really take a grip with the match fishing fraternity and to be really truthful we had no chance of winning against the Leeds lads or the Barnsley lads or any other lads come to think about it. Midway through the match and as I was falling asleep on the job I decided to go for a walk seeing as I wasn't catching much and about five pegs along I stopped behind former World Champion Dave Thomas.

'Do you mind if I sit behind you, Dave?' I asked. Well, if you're not catching there is no one better to sit behind than a World Champion but his answer totally threw me.

'YES I DO' ... Grumpy Mr Thomas didn't want any one sitting behind him. Oh well, but this little incident reminded me of a story about Noddy in Toyland who got kicked out for feeling grumpy ...

Back to Kent, back home and back to Kent again. I was the happiest bloke alive when they eventually paid me off. So it was back to Yarm and I was lucky to get voted onto Yarm AAs committee again. A lot had changed and there were a lot of new faces on the match scene. Young whipper snappers with the latest in pole technology and the expertise to use them were winning matches now and the matches seemed to be dominated by the pole. You can't make a pole from a shunting pole so I had to buy one as well and purchased a second hand 12.5 metre Browning Shimano from Brian Okeeffe who had purchased it from Ron Wilkinson who had only used it a few times so it was a bit of a bargain at the time. At the time there were regular matches run at Hemlington Lake in Middlesbrough but sadly since the cormorant deprivation of this once brilliant fishery these matches have been transferred to other venues. I hate cormorants. They are one of nature's ugliest and cruellest looking birds and their havoc, and decimation of fisheries has been well publicised but until someone with balls in the Government gets off his or her fat arse this pollution will continue to menace our fishing. Anyway it was time to get my head down again and try to catch up with methods and rigs that were in use now on the Tees. This was pre barrage days and to some extent the pole at Yarm was still in its infancy but you must flow with the times.

My little girl Kathryn was growing up and I sometimes took her along to catch some 'troach' or 'chubs' as she called them. For the first time Yarm AA didn't have a team in the Teesside League and to be fair the lads were getting a little bit sick of all the team fishing. We still entered the North East Winter League but since the demise of Yarm's famous team earlier in the eighties we hadn't fared at all well. We still haven't. We still travelled around a little to various matches but now stayed closer to home. The Ure at Ripon is still a cracking venue if you can get amongst the chub or barbel and the Swale still produces those big match weights but since the barrage was completed there is no reason to travel anywhere now.

It was in 1994 that I was first asked to be Match Secretary at Yarm and it was with much trepidation that I accepted. Being a match secretary at any club is daunting at the best of times but Yarm was going through a transition period when the attendances were very low and indeed some matches were being cancelled due to lack of participants. The task ahead was to put Yarm Angling Association back where it belonged at the top of the tree and I was very lucky to call on some very experienced club anglers who had seen their clubs falter in the past. The Tioxide bunch of Barry Smith, Davie Pearce, Keith Jones and Knocker Thorpe volunteered without hesitation, lads who I had enjoyed many a memorable coach trip with in years gone by, Martin Hobson and Geoff Douglas, two up and coming matchmen and the irrepressible Dave Rowden. Another dedicated organiser is Dave who some people find infuriating but to be honest if it wasn't for people like Dave the match fishing at Yarm would still be in the doldrums.

We set about the task of cutting out all of the pegs on all of Yarm AA's river water and this task is still going on even today. Every close season we set to with machetes, scythes and saws. We trimmed and cut and fell over and some times belted each other with bank sticks. More people would turn up every week with Tony Leeming and Dianne and the kids. Big Dick Sidgwick sometimes came and fell over as well, knocking his back out for weeks. Serves him right, he shouldn't have so far to fall ... Ginger John Youll is another welcome volunteer to the cause as John hates hogweed. For those of you who haven't been stung by these horrible plants that come a very close to cormorants on the hating scale, here's a little bit of advice, don't. They are horrible. They leave you with blisters that take for ever to go down if you are stung by them and are very dangerous.

Anyway the next priority was to get the match attendances up again and this involved reorganising the flow of people through Yarm's club house. At one stage the draw didn't start until everyone was in the club house and then we would draw at about nine o'clock. The reorganisation meant the utilising of the downstairs room which had a staircase that led upstairs into the bar.

Third job to consider was the bacon buttie situation and this is an area of expertise by my lovely wife, Lynda, who is better organised than I will ever be.

Fourthly advertising. The matches had to be advertised in the local press and the Nationals which is now something that we don't have to do as the matches are now very well attended. I was lucky in some respects that I was surrounded by people who were dedicated to the job and still are. Throughout the country whilst other club match attendances are dwindling Yarm AA is going from strength to strength and at this moment in time it is safe to say that the club and its stretch of water at Yarm is back where it belongs, at the top of the tree. The Tees barrage has helped enormously to put the fishing right at Yarm and it is a great pity that the team fishing has fallen so far back and another pity that the once good junior match fishing section has dwindled into oblivion, which is something that we are starting to address in both areas.

I have come a long way from those dark and dismal days at Port Clarence and the poverty and ringworm. Life has turned a full circle for me now and I am back where I belong in the North East of England but I now live in a rather picturesque part of the country with people who are my type of people. I have been just about everywhere and got all the tee shirts so the next time you see me just have a look and think to yourself, not bad for a little raggy arse from Port Clarence. To quote Colonel Nicholson when he stood on the bridge over the River Kwai as he talked to Colonel Saito the Japanese commander of the prisoners of war. 'You know, Colonel Saito, it's at times like this when you realise that you are nearer to the end than the start and you think to yourself, did your life make any difference at all?' and those immortal words of Colonel Saito... 'FAAAAAAAAARK OFF'.

To Graham Cox, Roger Ennefer and Speedy Leeming who never came back and to Tom Rivenberg who still suffers after all these years. To Phil Hicks who took a bullet for me and to all those others who suffered my indulgences, my tantrums and my passion for angling over the years, I can only say it was a pleasure to be there with you all. I wouldn't have changed any of it.

Epilogue

Over the past year the author of this book has undergone a period of mixed fortunes. Having qualified as a professional coarse angling instructor at Brooksby College, Melton Mowbray, he is now teaching his beloved sport in colleges and youth clubs in his native North East. His marriage has suffered and he is now going through a sad divorce with the woman whom he still loves. Almost as heartbreaking is the fact that he has discovered that his niece is suffering from an incurable mental disorder, something that has disturbed the author. He has penned a poem and has dedicated the words to his niece and to her mother, his sister.

The Sadness of Sophie

A sad little girl so lost and alone
In a whirlpool of memories that are never her own
And a Mother who's crying and torn up inside
With the anguish and sorrow that make-up can't hide.

A sad lonely girl who is haunted by doubt
At her Mother, a stranger, that she can't live without
Her comfort provider, her friend, yet her foe
When the voices inside her are telling her no.

When God chose his loved ones he beckoned her in
That radiant child bereft of all sin
A place is kept warming by his side just for her
That sad lonely girl, so special, so fair.

Her friends have long parted she suffers without
As the illness surrounds her, the voices, the doubt
And the calm that's her Mother, stands brave and so tall
The sadness of Sophie should live with us all.

To Christine for all your support and love.